To Andy from

S0-CFA-500

ART

ART

ERIC GILL

DEVIN - ADAIR
Publishers —— New York

This edition 1950

Made and printed in Great Britain by
WESTERN PRINTING SERVICES LTD. BRISTOL

Contents

5

" Without these the city is not built"

ECCLESIASTICUS XXXVIII

" The artist is not a special kind of man, but every man is a special kind of artist"

A. K. COOMARASWAMY

Preliminary

THIS book is written for people in general and not specially for those people called artists or those called connoisseurs and collectors. What is the thing or activity called art? What is it that connoisseurs collect? What are the things that connoisseurs do not collect? The world is so full of a number of things; what is this special thing called art? Is it a special thing? What is the difference between an "art" exhibition and an exhibition of motor cars? What is the difference between a beehive and the Tope of Sanchi or St. Paul's Cathedral? What is the difference between being artistic and being artful? In brief: what is art and does it matter?

In a book of this kind it is necessary to be absolutely clear. My appeal is to common sense. Rome is burning —at least the gunpowder is in the cellars—this is no time for dope. There is a thing called "bunk." It is not a nice thing; it is pretence, hypocrisy, make-believe. It is not necessarily malicious; the person who writes "bunk" may deceive himself. There is also a thing called "debunking." This is a most salutary activity. I wish to "debunk" Art.

The "debunking" of art is the more necessary at the present time because our industrialist commercial empire has achieved a thing never before achieved in the whole history of the world. It has achieved a division of the human race never before attempted—a division not of rich from poor, not of free from unfree, not of good from bad, clever from stupid but, unique marvel! a division of artist from workman. The division is now so complete that it is taken for granted. If I say: no workman is an artist, the retort is: of course not, no one expects him to be. No one expects him to be—that is the extraordinary thing. Art itself has become an extraordinary thing—the activity of peculiar people—people who become more and more peculiar as their activity becomes more and more extraordinary. And conversely, as work, that is to say the activity of workmen not artists, becomes more and more the activity of a kind of human ants, for industrialism has reduced the workman to a subhuman condition of intellectual irresponsibility, so the workman becomes less and less peculiar, more and more one of a herd taking its food, clothing, housing and amusement in tins, off tailors' dummies, by national housing schemes, from Hollywood and Broadcasting House.

There is a lot of bunk about work. There is a lot of bunk about art. I am only concerned to debunk art but, in passing, what a lot of bunk is talked and written about employment and unemployment! Manufacturers talk as though they wanted to employ people while all the time they are improving machinery so that they may save labour and thus do away with employment. Politicians talk about curing unemployment while all the time they are the obedient servants of the financiers who finance the manufacturers. And, on the other hand, the unemployed workman talks about wanting work when, like those who live on dividends and the proceeds of usury,

all he wants is money to buy things with.* The only
difference between "unemployment" and leisure is that
unemployment is leisure without the means to enjoy it.
Work! work is a curse and always has been. But until
our time the curse has been mitigated by the thing called
art. We have now separated art and work, cut them
right asunder and made foolishness of both.

We have got to be extraordinarily clear about all this.
What is art? What is work? And, indeed, what is man?
At bottom it is mistakes about man, misunderstandings
as to the kind of creature he is, that cause all the other
troubles. In a book about art man cannot but be
remembered; for though art, whatever way you look at
it, is the business of making things and it is the good of
the thing made that primarily concerns the artist as such,
nevertheless the things made are for men and it is men

---

* It is a fact that men are miserable if they have nothing to do. But
it remains certain that no unemployed industrial workman would take
employment if he had enough to live on without doing so. He would
employ himself; but that is quite a different thing. It is clear that idleness
is both wearisome and corrupting. This is as noticeable in Mayfair as
outside Labour Exchanges. But it is not true that any kind of labour is
preferable to idleness; it is only true that any kind of labour is preferable
to starvation. The only difference between work in a convict settlement
or an Army Labour Corps and work in a factory or as an employee of a
road-making contractor is that in the former you cannot be dismissed
or dismiss yourself whereas in the latter you are liable to "the sack" or
can go "on strike." But no one would to into such employment who was
not compelled either by law or by fear of death.

It may be asked: if these things be so, why do not "the unemployed"
occupy themselves in making things while they are "out of work"?
The answer is: that many do so employ themselves, and if the majority
do not it is because a century of industrialism has destroyed the initiative
for independent working. Most of them have not even the few pounds
required to buy the simplest tools and materials or to rent the smallest
workshop; nor could they sell what they made even if they could make it.
For one thing they are not allowed to do so while in receipt of "the
dole"; for another it is obviously impossible for them to compete with
the mass production of the factories.

A*

who make them. You cannot write about art as though it were an affair of angels, of purely spiritual beings. You cannot write about things as though they only existed in the imagination, as though they were bought by nobody and as though they were not made of material which somebody has to pay for.

There are special kinds of art which do not concern the man in the street just as there are special streets which do not concern the man in the studio. But this is not a book about any special kind of art or any special kind of man. It is about art in general and the things which every man needs. It is not only about paintings and sculptures but also about the furniture and utensils which everyone either makes or buys.

ERIC GILL

CHAPTER I

The Nature of Art

"Art embraces all making." All things made are works of art.

How are things made? What is necessary to the making of anything? First of all there is an idea in the mind. Second there is the material of which the thing is to be made. So far all is clear. You have an idea in your mind, material before you. What next? You take hold of that material, pull or push it about, cut it up, put several pieces together and so on—all according to the idea in your mind. How do you do these things? You use your hands and other people's hands, and those extensions of hands which we call tools and machines. In addition to the idea and the material, therefore, you require a third thing—call it tools, and in the word tools let us at this stage include hands and machines. But even so, more is required. It is not yet enough. It is not enough to have an idea and material and tools. To take hold of the material, to pull, to push, to cut, to join; what do all these verbs imply? There is a fourth thing necessary, without which ideas, materials, tools result in nothing. This fourth thing is the will to act. Confront a man with an idea; let it be supposed, if you will, that the idea is in his mind, it is something originating in him (never mind how at the moment); confront him with material; confront him

11

with tools; even so nothing made will result unless he wills to act. But a will to use the tools so that they are effective, so that the shape of the material conforms to the idea in the mind, implies more than the mere will. It is not sufficient to say: I will. It is necessary to say: I can; not only do I know what to do and how to do it but I have the ability to do it; I am able to do it; I have the skill to do it. The idea, the material, the tools, the will, the skill—all these things are necessary.*

I say art embraces all making and that therefore all things made are works of art. But what aspect of the thing made entitles it to the name art? A thing made is a work of art; but is it the idea in it that entitles it to be called art whether well made or ill made? Or is it the making which is the art whether the idea be good or bad? Is a good work of art one in which the idea is good whether the workmanship be skilful or clumsy, or is a good work of art one in which the workmanship is good whether the idea be wise or foolish?

This is the dilemma. Shall we, knowing that "art

---

* The existence of any thing has four *causes*:

  1. The defined purpose of the thing to be made (*Final Cause*.)
  2. The material of which the thing is made—for obviously different materials cause different results (*Material Cause*).
  3. The energy, force, will of the workman—for obviously, without these, purpose and material are insufficient (*Efficient Cause*).
  4. The imagination of the workman—for unless the workman sees the form of the thing to be made in his mind before he makes it, purpose, material and will can produce nothing (*Formal Cause*).

In the text the "idea in the mind" includes both the Final and Formal Causes. The material to be used is of course the Material Cause and tools, the will to act and skill in doing so are all divisions of the Efficient Cause.

abides entirely on the side of the mind,"* say, in the words of the song:

her mind, her mind is everything,

or, knowing that without skill, without at least a minimum of skill, nothing at all will be made, shall we say art is skill?

Here, as simple people, we shall find help in the ordinary usage of the common language. Art is skill, that is the first meaning of the word. That meaning underlies all others. From that sense of the word art all the derivatives come—artful, artisan, artificer, artificial, artistry. It is thus that we speak of the arts of cooking, of dentistry and of building, the art of logic and the art of the geometer. When we speak of the art of painting or the art of music or the art of the poet we are really using the word in the same sense, the sense of skill. We mean the ability to use paint, to make music, to put words together so that something is made—a picture, a symphony or a poem. But in these arts we are so conscious of their appeal to the intelligence, to the sensibility of intelligent beings, so conscious of the fact that they offer us nothing useful, that is to say nothing which ministers to our immediate physical convenience, that we entirely forget the skill of the workman who made the picture or music or poem and think of his work as having no real material existence. Then we are tempted to say art is not the skill of the workman; it is the act of the creative mind; and physical skill, the will and ability to use tools and the very material itself are inessential to the thing called art.

* Maratain, *Art and Scholasticism*, chap. 4, 3.

On the other hand I say that to make a drain pipe is as much the work of an artist as it is to make paintings or poems. The making of drain pipes is a different art from that of the painter of pictures. It is a different art, that is all. Art abides entirely on the side of the mind. Yes, and the idea of a drain pipe must be as clearly in the mind as the idea of a painting. There is no escape from mental responsibility. But the word art means skill: neither the painting nor the drain pipe would exist, either as pleasing objects or as useful ones, without the skill of their makers. All sorts of people have fine ideas, all sorts of people wish to serve their fellow-man by supplying them with things which please them or minister to their physical convenience, every man is potentially what is called an artist, but the fact remains, the artist is the person who actually has the skill and actually uses his skill to make things, to make, to bring into physical existence the things which abide in his mind. An artist is not simply a person with ideas. He is a person who has the skill to make his ideas manifest. He is not even a person with fine ideas or even fine skill; such a person is simply a better artist than others. Art itself is neither good nor bad; there is every kind of art, from the silliest and most inept to that which embodies the most refined sensibility in the most perfectly precise form.

Now this interpretation of the word art, founded though it be upon the original meaning of the word and in harmony with its use in common speech, might seem to lead to the conclusion that the best work of art is simply the most dexterous; that dexterity in workmanship, cleverness, *tour de force* and that sort of professional neatness which is called "trade finish" are the marks by which we may recognise the good work. Are such things art and, if so, what becomes of those works which while they seem to exhibit none of these marks, are yet objects of the highest reverence and which we purchase at great expense from those persons called art dealers and place in those houses specially called art galleries? If the skilful work is, on that account, the work of art, by what name shall we call these other things? If the engine of an airplane, the best paint brushes made by Winsor and Newton, a well-fitting chest of drawers, a well-tailored suit of clothes and a good tennis racket are works of art, and in the same sense of the word, how can the name art be equally justly applied to the idols of African negroes, the prinitive pottery of the land of Uz, the cave paintings of Ajanta and all the paintings of all the painters since the time of Raphael? Some of these works do indeed exhibit cleverness but that is not why we buy them or why we admire them. If the word art means skill, if skill in making is the very being of art what is the skill of the painter if it be not manual skill?

All art is skill in making; but there are many arts and many different kinds of skill. The skill required to design and construct the engine of a flying machine so that the flying machine will fly is of a different kind from that required by the painter so that he may make you see what he sees or feel what he feels. Both are art works; both demand skill but as their aims are different so are the kinds of skill required. In the case of the engineer the object is to construct something which will efficiently propel a carriage in the air. In the case of the painter the aim is to construct something which will efficiently propel an image, convey it from the painter's mind to that of the spectator even if the painter himself be the only spectator who will ever see his painting. In both cases the aim of the artist is to make something which will do something. In the case of the machine it is to do something to *things*. In the case of the painting it is to do something to *persons*.

In the case of the machine as such, and in all such cases, a high degree of technical dexterity is required in the artificers who do the work. Surfaces must be smooth, parts must fit exactly, measurement must be obeyed minutely, materials must be chosen, and tested to the last degree of science. It is only a secondary aim of the designer of machinery, if his machine be looked upon as a thing delightful to be seen—delightful as a thing harmonious in its physical shape—though a good machine may always be so looked at and is always a thing of beauty in the sense that the beautiful thing is that which pleases when seen. The object of the machine is to do something to another thing (in the case of an airplane it is to propel a carriage off the earth) and not to do anything to the spectator *qua* spectator. Its act is not spectacular though flying as an art performed by men may be so viewed.

In the case of the painting as such, and in all such cases, a high degree of dexterity is required, but in this case, it is not technical dexterity of the same kind as that required in the making of machines. For the act of the painter is not to do something to things but to do something to persons and, in such a case, surface polish and the exact fitting of parts by measurement with foot rules may not be either necessary or appropriate. The possibilities of materials, the nature of paint and of the stuff upon which the paint is to be laid must of course be explored and for these things a knowledge similar in kind to that needed by engineers is necessary; but this knowledge is acquired by the painter not in order that his painting may be effective but simply in order that it may endure. But as a machine may be worth looking at, so a painting may be effective upon things as a machine is effective—a thing moving other things, performing other physical acts than that of moving the mind of the spectator. A painting may be framed and used as a screen to keep off the cold draught of wind or the heat of the fire. In the form of woven tapestry it may be used as a wall-covering. As a postage stamp it may effect the lawful transmission of correspondence. As a thing over an altar it may show what God is worshipped in that place, thus being simply a vehicle of information and, like a notice board saying: this way to the Railway Station, effective like a machine, causing a movement of matter; for if the reredos portrays the image of Baal, the Christian, admitting himself to be in the wrong place, will go somewhere else, as the person seeking the Town Hall will be repelled by a direction to the Railway.

I say it is only secondary that the engine of a flying machine may be looked upon as a thing pleasing to sight. That it may be pleasing to the eye, pleasing to the mind of him who *sees* it, is not the first aim of the designer nor of the artificers who construct it. And it is only secondary that the things we call paintings may be used as machines, objects of physical utility, effective in any other way than as embodying the imaginations of their makers and making those imginations manifest. Nevertheless just as the good engine is always to be seen as a thing of beauty pleasing in itself, as though to be pleasing when seen were its first object, so the painting may always be used as a machine, an effective thing, effective as well as affective, and this not merely as a postage stamp, a wall-covering or a fire-screen but also as an educational agent, a means of conveying information, or simply a decoration, that is to say the appropriate treatment of the surface of things such that without that treatment the things are less useful, less efficient. Thus a carpet may be less useful as a floor-covering if it be plain and undecorated. A wall may be less satisfactory as the boundary of a living place if it be devoid of paintings or patterned wall-paper. For not only do plain carpets and plain walls show plainly every speck of dirt but the human mind is, normally, such that it demands the play of light and dark and colour and the normal man is positively miserable in such places as prison cells and the operating-theatres of hospitals where, for good reasons, paintings and decorations are inappropriate.

So all things made are works of art and, of art, skill is the *sine qua non*. There are different arts and therefore different kinds of skill. But if this is so, and if, as has been explained, there are two main divisions of art work —the arts whose business is to make things which affect other things and those whose business it is to effect other persons, the one to effect the movement of matter (as all tools and machines and objects of physical utility) the other to effect the motions of the mind (as all paintings and sculptures and music and poetry)—would it not be better to reserve the name of art definitely for one kind or the other and find or invent another name for the one not to be called art? Thus, in deference to the writers on painting and sculpture, the persons commonly called 'art' critics, we might reserve the name of art for all those arts whose sole business it is to affect the mind and we might call all other manufacturers something else.

What is the objection to this? There are two insuperable objections. First of all the just use of common speech forbids it. The word art does indeed mean skill. We cannot forbid such phrases as the art of cooking or the art of the pickpocket. We cannot deny that artful means "full of some kind of skill," that the artificer is some kind of skilful man and that the word artificial simply means "made by the deliberate skill of men," rather than by the instinctive operations of animals or the impersonal force of inorganic nature, and does not necessarily imply anything to do with those works whose object is to make manifest the ideas and imaginations of painters and sculptors, musicians and poets.

The second objection is even more overwhelming. It is this: that there is in fact no hard and fast division and separation between the two kinds of art. It is not normal to men to make even machines without paying some attention to the fact that machines are seen and heard and touched as well as used. Even though the designer of airplane engines thinks very little of the appearance of his mechanism, it is obvious that this thoughtlessness is not characteristic of the designer of locomotives, still less of the designers of carts and carriages, of fountain-pens and foot-warmers, of fire-escapes and frying-pans. All these persons, these artists, however much their economic reward depends upon their attention to physical serviceableness, are concerned for the appearance of the things they make.* Still more obvious is this in the case of the building and furnishing arts. Who can deny that building is an art which touches at every point both the sphere of physical utility and the sphere of the affections? How can we say that building only becomes an art when it ceases to be useful, in face of the fact that the only bad buildings are those in which a reasonable notion of utility is flouted or denied and the fact that the vast majority of buildings are definitely useful and erected primarily to be used.

On the other hand it is not normal to man to make even pictures and sculptures without regard to the fact that pictures and sculptures must be placed somewhere and must therefore be either suitable or unsuitable in that place, appropriate or inappropriate, seemly or unseemly, right or wrong, a blessing or a nuisance. And, whatever painters and sculptors may think about it or critics write, the economics of the matter make it clear that the idea of service is inseparable from the idea of art. However pure the intentions of the painter may be, however unalloyed, however free he may be from any motive but that of embodying a representation of his own spiritual state without thought of doing good to his neighbour or decorating his neighbour's drawing-room, it remains obvious that no one can buy things that they have not, as they say, "got a use" for. "What," the possible purchaser may ask, "is the good of my buying this painting? I shouldn't know what to do with it," or "I haven't anywhere to put it."

Moreover, it is only in rare epochs of human life that

* i.e., They realize that the things they make are also objects to be contemplated as beings and not merely as instruments.

such a question ever arises. The question whether the name of art is only rightly applied to things whose sole purpose is the delight of the mind and is wrongly applied to things which by definition are objects of utility, such a question cannot normally be asked. For though it is, in theory, possible to make a machine which no one will ever see and though it is possible, in theory, to put a picture on a wall without paying any regard to its surroundings, these things are so rarely done that they may justly be regarded as humanly abnormal, eccentric and monstrous. Painting is primarily the art of decorating with paint (hence of course the trade of the "painter and decorator"—not because painting and decorating are different things but because they always go together). Decorating is the art of making buildings and other things more habitable, more suitable to the purposes for which they were made. It is not primarily an art of self-expression, of spiritual exhibitionism. A painting is not primarily a "performance," a thing like a child's piece of recitation, a thing which the painter does like a mountebank or a conjurer. There are such paintings and they have their proper place and occasion—the museum called the picture gallery or, at home, a cupboard from which we can take them from time to time to look at them as at rare and precious and delightful curiosities—but, primarily, the business of painting is the business of making decorations in paint and, as the word decoration suggests, the business of painting is inseparable from ideas of what is right and proper, decorous and seemly. The painter renders a service. It is a service of doing in paint what is rightly done in the place where painting should rightly go.

So it is with all the arts, and the distinction is not between art and skill or between art and utility as though we were distinguishing between spirit and matter or between soul and body; for art and skill are the same thing and all arts are in a proper sense useful arts. The distinction is simply between those arts which serve the body and those which serve the mind. And as, in man, spirit and matter, the useful and the entertaining, the idea and its embodiment are inseparable, so it is common to find those things most delightful which by definition are simply objects of utility and those things most useful which by definition are simply entertaining. In fact it may well be said that the most useful art is that of entertainment; for there is no point in entertainment unless it be in some way health-giving to our souls; whereas a house is worse than useless if you cannot bear the sight of it; for there is no point in a shelter if it only makes you miserable. In the long run man only wants to be happy. What makes him happy is useful; and what does not make him happy is, in quite a short run, useless.

We may say that the idea in the mind and the paint under a magnifying glass are different things. But when we see a picture we do not see the idea and the paint separately. If we see the paint as a chemist might see it we are not seeing the picture. If we see the idea as a philosopher or a psychologist might see it we are not seeing the picture. It is precisely the same with an engine. We may say that the function of the machine and the metal of which it is made are different things. But when we see the machine we do not see the function and the metal separately. If we see the metal as a metallurgist might see it we are not seeing the machine.

If we see the function as a lexicographer might see it we are not seeing the machine.

But we cannot thus separate art and skill. We cannot say such and such would be a good machine if it were better made or such and such is a bad picture but well painted. We can say such and such is a bad machine but beautifully polished and we can say that such and such is a good picture but its painter knows nothing of perspective, has never studied anatomy and has no better tool than a toothbrush. But there is no such thing as a good machine badly made. If it be not well made it is not a good machine. And there is no such thing as a good picture badly executed. For the execution of the thing is our only means of knowing it and if we can really say that such and such a thing is badly made then we are really saying that it was a bad thing to make. The maker himself does not fully know his own conception until he has executed it, and the man in the street cannot know it at all until he sees the work before him. The relation between the image in the mind of the maker and the executed work is one of more or less complete identity —more complete in the case of phsyically useful things, less complete in that of objects whose usefulness is spiritual. The reason of this is that the final cause, the end of the work, in the case of the physically useful object is more defined and, being defined, its limits are easily recognised and can be perceived by one sweep of the mind. But in the case of paintings, sculptures, music and poetry the limits being spiritual are less easily discernible.*

* It is not my intention here to make any distinction between mental and psychological and spiritual. My dictionary says psychology is the science of the human soul or mind—that is to say, either or both, implying that they are the same thing. Let it be so here.

The mechanician who polishes what ought not to be polished is a bad mechanician though he be a good polisher. The painter who depicts anatomy which is irrelevant to his picture is a bad painter though he be a fellow of the Royal College of Surgeons. The maker of pins who omits their points is not a maker of pins. The point about a pin is its point—you cannot have a pin without a point any more than you can think of such a thing. The painter who depicts Venus with a beard is not a painter of Venus even though he label the picture with letters a yard high. It is no use kicking a cricket ball, however hard you do it, even though you kick it over the "boundary," and to hit a football with your walking stick does not make you a cricketer. Skill is always relevant to the job in hand.

Nevertheless a painter may have acquired the skill to wield a paint brush in a manner consonant with the nature of paint brushes and yet have no pictures in his head; and a man may have a head full of pictures and rheumatism in his finger-joints. And sometimes a child, because it has long fingers, is coerced by its parents into playing the piano. Even so art is skill; for the person who can wield a paint brush may indeed follow the art of painting even if he cannot follow that of painting pictures. The only difficulty is that of discovering what place or occasion is most suitable to his talent. The man of imagination whose hands fail him can still achieve his pictures though with more pain and labour. And the child with long fingers, though it may never do more than play scales and exercises, can at least do scales and exercises as they should be done. You cannot play good music badly. If you do not play it as it should be played you are not playing it at all—there is no such thing as good playing except of good music.

But surely, it may be urged, it is possible to have bad designs well built, or, conversely, bad building of good designs. No, neither alternative is possible and experience shows this clearly. How can you have a good building badly built or a bad building well made? What could well made mean in such a case? How can bad meat be well cooked? What sort of cooking can be applied to bad meat that we could call the result good?

Or, you may ask, cannot there be a bad reproduction of a good painting? In such a case may we not say that the idea was good but the execution faulty? Neither can this be allowed. For the reproduction, though it be labelled and sold and thought of as such, is itself an original work. Though made by the hundred, reproductions are handed out one by one. They are seen one by one. Your reproduction of the Sixtine Madonna by Raphael is, for you, a painting of the Madonna. As it hangs on your wall it is either as a thing on your wall ought to be or it is not. The man who made it with his camera and his commercial organisation is in exactly the same position as a man writing a poem. A poet, in spite of all the Victorian critics, cannot say to himself: I have an idea for a poem about "my Julia's leg," and then go on to ask himself whether it would be better in iambics or hendecasyllabics. The poem has the form it has—in a different form it would be a different poem. So it is with your reproduction manufacturer; good, bad or indifferent, he must see the thing whole. The idea of a reproduction of the Sixtine Madonna, as soon as it is imagined is a thing imagined in paper or tin or gelatine.

It is a work of art, however thoroughly nauseating. The painting by Raphael may have given the manufacturer his idea, just as Julia's leg inspired Robert Herrick, but the reproduction was the manufacturer's own idea and whether the original Raphael be good or bad does not make any difference to the responsibility of the maker of reproductions.*

So it is also with all machine-made things. The fact that they are or may be made by the thousand is a controlling condition. To imagine a button-hook as made out of bent wire with your own elegant fingers is to imagine a certain kind of button-hook. To imagine a button-hook as made by the dozen by a machine is to imagine another kind of button-hook altogether. The designer of things to be made by machinery is a different kind of artist from him who makes things, as they say, by hand. Factory designers are only just beginning to find this out, but they are now finding it out. They are finding out that the badness of Victorian machine-made things was not at all that they were good designs badly made, or bad designs excellently machined, but that they were not imagined as machine-made things at all. Their designers, like the first printers, were unable to shake off the traditions, conventions, fashions and fal-lals of their predecessors. They thought, to use the jargon of art-

* What we call a bad reproduction may really be bad only in its label. If it professes to be a facsimile of something else and is not a facsimile, though its label says so, then the label is wrong. But the reproduction, though wrongly labelled, is good or bad *in itself*. Thus there is in many Catholic churches a picture called "Our Lady of Perpetual Succour." It is supposed to be a reproduction of a picture in Rome. The reproductions vary widely; no two are alike. The only error any one makes is in supposing them to be facsimiles. Many of them are good things in themselves, many are bad. Some may be better than the original. Who knows?

criticism, that "form and content" could be separated. Like the bad poet who finds it necessary and thinks it possible to choose between one metre or another, or like the Royal Academy sculptor who thinks a statue can be modelled in clay and that, after that, it does not much matter whether it be cast in bronze or mechanically copied in marble, so the machine-facturer designed things according to pre-industrial ideas and foolishly thought it possible to make them by machinery.

But, again it may be urged, you can have a good book badly printed, or the worst poem in the world exhibiting the highest art of the typographer. This is true; but in such cases there is clearly the combination of two arts. Let us separate them. There is the art of writing and the art of printing. Let us take the art of writing (by which of course I do not mean that of the calligrapher, but that of the artificer of words, the art of verbiage); as before, I say you cannot have a bad book well written; you cannot have bad ideas in good language. There is no such thing as good language for the expression of bad notions; there is no such thing as bad language for good ideas; a good idea cannot be expressed in bad words or in bad grammar or in bad style. A good thought, if it exist in words at all must be in good words; no other kind is possible. But again we may be unconsciously combining and confusing two separate arts. There is the art of the thinker and that of the grammarian; these are indeed twain though they may become one flesh. It is only a kind of snobbery to assume that the grammarian's grammar is always and everywhere essential to the man of letters. It is the same kind of snobbery as that in which it is assumed that no gentleman can go unshaved

or do any of the things which "no fellow should do."
The sabbath was made for man not man for the sabbath
and not every day of the week is a Sunday. The art of
the grammarian exists, like that of the logician or the
polisher of piston-rods, for certain definite occasions and
purposes. It would be as absurd to say that an expression
of thought must always be in the form of subject, predi-
cate and object, as to say that all boots must be polished,
all lettering constructed on the model of the Trajan
inscription or all type faces designed on the basis of handwriting.

And take the art of typography. Is it not possible to
print good type badly or to make a good impression of
a bad face of type? But here again two separate arts are
confused. The art of the designer of printing type is a
different art from that of the printer of books. Obviously
it would be well if the two were in league. Obviously the
designer of types must be intimately acquainted with the
art of printing. Nevertheless printing is no more the
same art as letter designing than letter drawing is the
same art as punch cutting. The punch cutter cannot cut
a good letter badly; if he cuts a bad letter it is only
because he has a bad letter in his head. If the designer
draws bad letters it is only because he does not know a
good letter when he sees one. If the printer prints badly
it is only because he has a bad notion of printing. Of
course the potter's hand may shake and an earthquake
may shake the hands of all the workmen at once. Conversely there are many steady hands at Stoke-on-Trent
and yet an annual output of millions of bad pots.

But it may be said, no one is complaining about *lack*
of skill. No one is saying sleight of hand is necessary to

the painter of pictures or that primitive pottery exhibiting the handiwork of very shaky potters is not as good or better than the product of the most up-to-date machinery. The trouble, it may be said, is exactly the opposite. The contention is not that lack of technical precision causes the production of bad works but that its presence does not cause the production of good ones. We do not mind, they say, whether things are neatly finished or not; we do not mind about perspective or anatomical verisimilitude; we do not mind whether teacups are exactly round or exactly oval in shape; we do not mind whether an artist is as clever as a conjurer or as clumsy as a bear. What we object to is the notion that art is skill and that material finish or precision has anything to do with it.

The confusion of mind here is a confusion between the notions of doing and making and a confusion between doing deeds and making things. Art is skill; but it is skill in *making*. It is not mere dexterity; it is dexterity directed towards making. The business of the pickpocket is called an *art* when we regard the business not simply as that of extracting coins from pockets unbeknown, but when we regard the pickpocket as making a nice job of it —when we can see the act as a thing made. The act of the artist is not a prudential act. It is an act directed to the good of the thing to be made.

Skill in making, the thing called art, degenerates into mere dexterity, i.e. skill in doing, when the workman, for whatever reason or under whatever compulsion or in whatever state of social or physical or spiritual or political or economic degradation, ceases to be concerned, for the thing made or, having become a mere tool, a "hand" in the employ of another, has no longer any responsibility for the thing made and has therefore lost the knowledge of what it is that he is making. Do the potters at Stoke-on-Trent know what they are making? In many factories the "hands" cannot even know what they are *supposed* to be making. All their acts are deeds. All their acts are prudential acts. They polish this or twist the other simply because they are told to do so. They obey because their wage depends on it and they depend on their wage. The factory hand can only know what he is *doing*. What is being made is no concern of his.

And it is the same with many other workmen, even when they are not the victims of industrialism. Art is skill in making; but the thing to be made must first of all be known in the mind. If it be not known in the mind it is obvious that no degree of surface finish or juggling with tools will bring it into existence. The trouble in those times and places where technical dexterity takes the place of skill in making is not at all in the fact of technical dexterity for dexterity is in itself a good. The trouble is simply the degradation of the mind. In such times and places the artist, the responsible workman is without clear ideas and without desire. He does not know what he is making; he does not see it clearly in his mind or he does not desire above all things to make it. He falls back upon mere dexterity. His polishing and smoothing and fitting and neatness, his attention to anatomy and the laws of chiaroscuro are all prudential acts; they are not really directed towards the good of the work, but towards the soothing of his conscience or the satisfaction of his master. . . .

Art is skill in making; the good work is the skilful

work, the work in which the apporpriate means have been employed to effect the desired end. If inappropriate means have been employed, the end will not, cannot be achieved. Everything depends upon the nature of the end desired and ends are many and various. It is obvious that the workman must know what he wants to make before he begins the work; it is equally obvious that he must be able to make it or the thing will not be made. Knowing what is to be made is one thing, and knowledge is a thing which may be acquired by anyone; it is connatural to man to know what he desires and all men in consequence are potentially artists; but the word art means skill in making and the name of artist is reserved to him who has the skill to make things and does actually make them.

CHAPTER II

Before 1500

ALTHOUGH the word art is to-day commonly spelt with a capital A this has not always been so. It was the peculiar achievement of the nineteenth century to separate, in thought and in practice, the idea of work from the idea of art, the activity of the "workman" from the activity of the "artist," and to make the artist a special person, removed from and exalted above the common ruck of human beings, a sort of priest, the expert in a mystery, a mystery not of craft or trade unionism but of spiritual remoteness. He was allowed a different morality to correspond with his detachment from ordinary people. If one law for the lion and the ass is a tyranny, as William Blake proclaimed, one law for artists and men of business or clergymen of the Church of England became equally monstrous. The notions of work, the object of working and its reward, which moved the makers of industrial England were so obviously different from the notions which moved those workmen who had escaped the world of commerce and the factory, or who by temper or inclination were unable to enter it, that it was impossible that their morals should not be different also.

But this difference of life and morals is not the important thing here. The theme of this book is art in the twentieth century. In order to understand the position of art and the arts to-day we must understand their

position in the past and first of all we must understand
their position before what we call the modern world
emerged from the rule of princes and ecclesiastics into the
domination of merchants and financiers and manufacturers. This birth or emergence occurred about four
hundred years ago. Before that time (let us call it
approximately the year 1500) there was no such class of
workmen as those we call artists. There were of course
painters of pictures and carvers of images. There were
makers of songs. There was a high and venerable development of music and especially melody. There was,
pre-eminently, a grand tradition of building—though by
the year 1500 this tradition had succumbed to the domination of contractors and of builders' merchants and was
frittering itself away in structural ostentation and that
sumptuous repetition of ornaments which merchants
always love. There were writers of chronicles, philosophers, poets, vernacular singers and story-tellers and
writers on theology and spiritual matters in abundance
in spite of war, pestilence and famine, battle, murder and
sudden death; but there were no artists as we have them
to-day. There were no gentlemen workmen. There was
no class distinction between the painter of pictures and
the painter of door-posts, between the poet and the
common man. There was distinction of function but not
distinction of class. The bricklayer to-day may think
himself and may be a higher kind of workman than his
labourer. He may indulge in a great deal of trade snobbery; but they are both of the same social class. But
before the year 1500, or thereabouts, the same might be
said of the sculptor and the mason. They were a higher
or lower grade of workman, but there was no social dis-

B

tinction between them. You could not say one was a gentleman and the other not.

And just as there was no gentleman painter so there was no gentleman architect. The architect was the builder, the man who did the work, the man who employed the various tradesmen. He was a tradesman himself. He went in at the tradesman's entrance. He had risen from the workshop, he had not come down from the university. The university was not the finishing school for gentlemen (though, of course, there is no earthly reason why gentlemen should not be finished); it was the training school for clerks, that is to say for clerics and all the numerous ecclesiastics and lawyers who needed, in order to do their jobs, a clerical, that is to say a literary education.

The architect was the builder; he was the head of the building gang. His training and apprenticeship were obtained on the job, on the scaffold, in the mason's yard or the carpenter's shop or the plumber's. He was called "master builder" not because he was master of men but because he was master of his trade and knew the traditions.

The thing which, in the twentieth century, we call art was unknown to builders before the year 1500. It was unknown to their customers and it was unknown to the men who worked with them. But this does not mean that it did not exist. It only means that it was not talked about or thought about as a thing other than the job in hand. To build a church was to build a church, not a sample of architecture. To carve a statue of a king was to carve a statue of that king and not to make a sample of sculpture, an essay in "the relations of masses."

To make a toasting-fork was to make a toasting-fork, not a sample of artistic ironwork. To invent a chant for the Mass was to invent a chant for the Mass, not to make a musical composition. And this is not to say that what we in the twentieth century call art is a bad thing or that we in the twentieth century always fail to make good buildings or good statues or good fire-irons or good music for churches; good or bad is not in question here. I am only saying that such and such was the way they looked at it before the year 1500 and that their way of looking at things was the common way throughout the world, as the normal way for men to look at the business of making things and is not our way. Whether we make better things or worse than they did is not the question here; but we may note that by common agreement we preserve their buildings, and even the ruins of their buildings, as architectural monuments and take architect's pupils to look at them; we take their statues and put them in glass cases in our museums as admirable examples of sculpture; we collect their ironwork and weep over its beauty and we make gramophone records of their chant as samples of admirable melody.

The architect was the builder, even when, as sometimes happened, he was the pet of his patrons. The architect was the builder; he knew about building. He knew nothing about any other style of building but the one he was brought up to practise. In this respect he was very much like a modern engineer. What do modern engineers know about any engineering but their own? Can there be, in the engineer's mind, any other style of flying machine worth knowing about or worth making but the latest style, the one he is himself trying to improve upon? Can there be, in the mind of the engineer of iron bridges, any other style of iron building worth thinking about but the one which we have now at this moment arrived at? Is it conceivable that, fascinated by the elegant appearance of the Clifton suspension bridge, any engineer would propose or any town council accept a bridge of that sort to-day?

So it was with builders and architects, if we like the word (it only means ruler of workmen), before the year 1500. They did not build according to gentlemanly notions of style. They built according to the traditions of the trade, traditions constantly changing, welcoming every new dodge or improvement but never going back to earlier and, as they thought, outworn methods of building or styles of ornamentation.*

So it was with all other trades. Painting and sculpture were trades. If the word art was used at all it was used in its proper meaning—skill, the skill of the workman, the skill of the workman as a maker of things. The painting of pictures was simply the highest grade of painting and decorating. The painter of pictures started life in the workshop of the painter and decorator. He started as an apprentice to the trade. He began by learning how to grind and mix pigments just as an apprentice to painting and decorating does to-day. But before the year 1500 there was nothing else that a person with a talent for painting pictures could do. There was no such thing as art as a thing independent of and superior to the common necessities and the common

---

* I say "never going back"; that was the general rule. But archæologians can bring forward a few freak exceptions and they are welcome to do so.

work of the time and there was, of course, no such thing as an art school. You could not have asked any ordinary person, any person not a philosopher, what art was. He would simply have said: what art? There was no such thing in their minds as art by itself—a special line of business. There was only this art or that art—the art of cooking, the art of logic, the art of sculpture . . . and all arts were thought of simply as being the different kinds of skill which different kinds of necessities demanded. The art of the bootmaker grew from the people's need of boots, that of the mason from their need of buildings, that of the sculptor from their need of images.

And, such is the nature of man, it is often difficult to distinguish between art and prudence. You make a wall with a hole in it to let in the air. But the hole has to be shaped this way or that—with an arch or a lintel. The job of making it is interesting in itself. The act of prudence becomes the work of art, the act of making a *thing*, a thing worth making for its own sake and, if made according to reason and according to the sensibilities of a rational being, a thing pleasing to the eye, pleasing to the mind, a thing of beauty. Men acting according to their nature can hardly do an act of prudence without making an art of it.

As buildings got bigger, that is to say as men prospered and established themselves in security, the idea of a window as being chiefly a means of ventilation gave way to the idea of a window as being chiefly a means of light. Therefore it was filled with glass to keep out the wind. But glass is not naturally or easily made of uniform whiteness and translucency. The idea of coloured windows was unavoidable. To find pleasure in pattern, a pattern of colours and shapes rhyming together, is as natural as it is to find displeasure in discords or noises which set the teeth on edge. How could the window-maker not arrange his bits of coloured glass in some sort of order?

From patterns to pictures is an obvious road even though it be a long one. And pictures themselves are an intricate tangle of art and prudence. In a window or on a wall what picture is appropriate? The painter alone could not decide. Even if he had wished to do so he would not have been allowed to. For who will pay for the picture? The painter did not paint pictures for his health but to the order of his customers; and who will pay money, who has ever paid money or ever will, unless he gets what he wants.

There is of course a reasonable give and take. The reasonable customer knows that there are things about the art of painting which he knows nothing about. In such matters the painter has his way. But the reasonable painter knows that, as he takes his customer's money, he is the servant of his customer and must in justice supply what his customer asks for. The art and prudence of painting pictures therefore are matters decided between the workman and the buyer. Painting is not something done simply to please the eye of the painter; it is also something done to please the customer. The building is presumably the customer's property. The decision as to what kind of picture is to be painted on its walls or in its windows must rest with him. The painter cannot give him Venus if he demands St. James. Nor can he omit St. James and give him simple arabesques. He cannot say to his customer: I am here to exhibit the quality of my soul, the fineness of my spirit, the lusciousness of my sensibility—I am here to show myself off—my sort of art is, at bottom, self-expression, the expression of my artistic self; it is in fact spiritual exhibitionism. He cannot say such things, not before the year 1500. There is no money in it a (phrase of the twentieth century, but in a sense less disgusting than that in which advertisers use it) and it is your money he wants (another modern phrase, a phrase not used by advertisers), wants, that is to say needs. Painting is a means of livelihood, just as making boots is. There is, before the year 1500, no high-faluting nonsense about the business, no art-nonsense in fact. The painter is a tradesman—a high-class tradesman, high enough sometimes to be the friend of princes, but never a gentleman, never a person of independent means, never a person who thinks his job is simply to please himself, though there is no reason to suppose he was never pleased by it. He is never a person who thinks he knows better what his customer ought to have than his customer knows himself, and, above all, he is never a person who thinks that the art of painting has nothing to do with being useful, making useful things, as though he were not a man like his customer and as much concerned with prudence as any one else.

And as there is no art-nonsense about painting before the year 1500, so there is not necessarily any improper servility. The painter is not a mere tool or "hand" caught in the net of a degrading industrialism. There is fair give and take. The customer does not fancy himself as a person of superior sensibility. He wants a certain thing or a certain kind of thing and he goes to the kind of person capable of giving it to him. He does not tell the painter how to paint but only what he wants painted. Generally the painter is not a person working independently of the rest of the building gang. Generally he is called in by the builder just as the 'painter and decorator' is called in in this twentieth century. The masonry or brickwork is finished; what shall we do about the painting and decorating? And there is no business about signing the work, except for fun and in secret; for no one cares particularly who did it as long as it is done and no one thinks of the work as having any special value because it is the work of John rather than that of James. If anyone gets any of the pride of self-expression out of it, it is more likely to be the customer than the workman. William of Wickham built or rebuilt the cathedral of Winchester. Bishop Storey built the market cross at Chichester. St. Louis, King of France, built the holy chapel at Paris. William of Normandy built the Tower of London. It is only by an elaborate and patient sort of prying that we can discover the names of any actual workman and seldom is it possible to say this or this is the actual work they did.*

I say that before the year 1500 there is not necessarily any improper servility. There was nothing in the way of working, or in the relations between employers and employed prevailing in pre-commercial centuries, which made work servile in itself or employers into slave masters. If there was injustice it was due to sin and not to the system. If there was cruelty it was the fault of bad men and not the blind working of any economic

* See Appendix I.

laws. If there was much routine work it was because there were many for whom routine work was the kind of work they could do best.

Moreover, it should be noted, the thing called routine work, the miles of moulding, the thousands of repeated ornaments, increases in quantity as we approach the end of the pre-commercial period. For there was no sudden break. The year 1500 does not mark a sudden change from the dark of medievalism to the light of modernity. 1500 is only a date. But there is dawn before sunrise and even at night it is never wholly dark. There is gestation before birth and the baby we have produced was certainly conceived long before. The routine work put into the nave of Westminster Abbey, though much less than that put into the chapel of Henry the Seventh (a remarkable exhibition of mercantile grandiosity), is much more than that to be found in buildings of a century or two centuries earlier.

But, in their way of working, even routine work was necessarily very different from what it has become under a system of machine and mass production. There are perhaps more than a thousand feet of moulded stone in the arches of the nave of Westminster Abbey, all cut from the same pattern or template. There are hundreds of feet of simple pattern work—mere repetition as far as a cursory glance can show. There are many thousands of stones for walling of which the most that can be said is that they are cut fair and square, that is to say fair and fit (*pulchro et bono* as St. Augustine puts it). But even for such work, and there was much of it, the individual workman was compelled by the nature of the conditions under which he worked (the absence of cheap

B*

drawing-paper upon which to set out full size, as architects do to-day, the exact details—the absence of sawing machinery so that much contrivance had to be employed to make the most economical use of stone—the fact that, whatever had to be done, some man had to do it, some human being, with his own hands and only the simplest tools), the workman was compelled to use his intelligence, however little he had, not merely as a person doing what he was told but as a person making what he intended to make. He was not minding a machine which made things, but making things because he intended to make them. He may have been poor, down-trodden, underpaid and verminous; miserable as regards the cruelty of his employer and rebellious as regards the extortions of barons and bishops, but he was not a mere tooth on a wheel, a mere "hand," simply because he could not be; there was no possibility of making him such.

Such was the state of what we now call the art world before the sixteenth century. Such indeed has been the art world through human history and in all the countries of the world except in peculiar times such as our own and except in such peculiar places as the galleries and salons of a commercially dominated Rome or London.

For there is nothing particularly medieval in the notion that the artist is simply the responsible workman, the man who makes things, the skilful man. I do not cite the Middle Ages because they were good ages or because, in those ages, a certain set of ideas were held to be just and seemly. I do not "cite" them at all. I am merely describing the sort of attitude towards work and towards art-work which was taken in the age preceding our own.

And the division between our age and that which went before it is not to be seen first of all in the fact that we in our own time regard work in one way and they in theirs regarded it in another. The primary difference is one of government. We enjoy the rule of bankers and money-lenders; they suffered under the yoke of princes and ecclesiastics. We regard trading as the most beneficent enthusiasm which can enthral the minds of men; they kept or tried to keep the traders subordinate, believing that avarice and usury and the trickery of men of business were, of all things, the most mean and harmful to the State, and holding that the business of government was in some way holy and that authority, from that of the kings and princes down to the authority of a father over his chlid, was derived from God. It is our different idea of government which chiefly marks off the modern world from the world of medieval kings.

But with such a different notion of government it is inevitable that all other notions should differ also. In times and places wherein trading was kept in subordination and traders regarded as dangerous men, men who, if not watched, would undoubtedly destroy the peace, corrupt men and degrade them, it was inevitable that there should be a way of working different from ours and that the relations between the workman and his customer should be different.

I do not say in this place whether such a way of working or whether such a relationship was better or worse. The point here is that work and the relations between men were different, and it is that difference I am insisting upon.

Whether better or worse does not matter the at

moment but it would be well to repeat, before passing
to the modern world, that the way of working which
prevailed in medieval Europe and the relation between
lords and masters on the one hand and men and workmen on the other which medieval polity and piety sought
to preserve and develop, was in harmony with what so
great a majority of men has always held to be man's
nature. Man, they held, is a responsible being. He is
responsible for his acts and for the intended consequences of his acts. He is responsible for his work and
for the quality of it. He is a creature who can be praised
or blamed. The artist, they held, is the skilled workman.
His business is to make what is wanted for those who
want it. The beautiful thing, they held, is that which
being seen pleases; and they did not dream of the possibility of useful articles being anything but beautiful or
of the possibility of beauty being divorced from usefulness. The idea of work, the idea of art, the idea of
service and the idea of beauty were and are, in spite of
our peculiar century, naturally inseparable; and our
century is only peculiar in that we have achieved their
unnatural separation.

CHAPTER III

1500–1900

THE chief difference between the world before about the year 1500, the medieval world, and the world since that date, the world which we still call "modern," is in the matter of government. It is not that a change of government is the prime cause and that religion, climate, geographical discovery and many other things are not antecedent to political change but when we take note of the differences between the modern world and the world which preceded it and wish to discover the most important and vital difference, the difference which bears most materially upon the matter of human work and the matter of human art, the matter of this book, the most important matter in the world—the things men do and make (for by their fruits you shall know them)—we shall find that it is the difference between the kind of government we have got and the kind they had before.

It is not that the change in government was complete; for the rule under which we now labour, and under which many millions groan, is even now neither completely secure nor universally accepted. And it was the same in the preceding centuries. Princes and churchmen, now more or less impotent, were, even when they were most powerful, never omnipotent. Insurrection and disorder were as common in the political history of those

Nor is it that the change in government was a sudden one; for no particular year can be named as that in

which the old rule was overthrown and the new one
substituted. Political forms overlap. Religious ideas
spread more rapidly or decay more rapidly in one place
than another. Corruption assails one court while another
remains pure. Resistance to chance is more stubborn
here than there. You cannot say: here is the perfect and
complete example of theocracy or there is the perfect
specimen of a peasant society uncorrupted by foreign
trade or the tyranny of landlordism. You cannot say:
up to this year the country was democratic in its institutions and in the next year it was oligarchic. Nothing is
ever completely itself nor is anything ever changed all
at once.

Nevertheless it is only by a sort of cowardice that we
refuse to make decisions and to name things. A rose
may be covered by green-fly; but it would be a timid
sort of naturalist who refused to decide what the thing
he saw was, and refused to name the thing a rose in spite
of the fly. There were money-lenders in England in the
thirteenth century; but they did not rule. There are
kings in the twentieth; but they rule no longer. The
Middle Ages were monarchical, feudal and religious, and
sought by every kind of legal contrivance to keep the
mere trader subordinate. The nineteenth century was
oligarchic, individualistic and religiously undecided and
sought by every kind of legal device to make the organ
of government, the parliament, subservient to the
ambitions of men of commerce and money-lenders.
Money-lenders often succeeded in medieval Europe in
bringing off fine coups. Men of nobility and disinterested
mind have not been altogether unsuccessful in modern
England in effecting fine measures of social amelioration

in face of the opposition of all the vested interests. But in spite of these things, these confusions, these over-layings of one thing by another, these insurrections and disorders, in spite of these things we know the nature of the time we live in and can name it. We know the difference between the modern world and its predecessor. We know a date before which the general note was different from that sounded afterwards. However ano-malous the borderland may be we know when we are in England and not in Wales. We know that, with the fall of the Plantagenets, the rule of the kings, in spite of the grandeur of the Tudors, was doomed. We know that the spiritual power of the church, in spite of her possession of Papal States, was broken, that the rule of money, in spite of the romantic buccaneering of the Elizabethan pirates and, later . the spiritual buccaneering of the Cromwellian puritans had begun.

In this business of discerning the function of art in the modern world and the position of the arts, these things must be put first. It is not a matter of politics as we understand the word, it is a matter of politics as the word ought to be understood. Who shall rule? What ideas shall be paramount? What is man? Is he a responsible being and, if so, should it not be the function of government to preserve and encourage that responsi-bility to the utmost? What is art? Is it the business of tickling the fancy of the rich by supplying them with what they naturally like best, portraits of themselves and pictures of their possessions and both portraits and pictures as nearly resembling the appearance of things as may be? Or is it the business of making in general and, more particularly, the well-making of what needs making? Is the idea of good to be what will sell or is it to be that which is in conformity with the nature of responsible beings, beings for whom, because they are in an absolute sense responsible, holiness is the ultimate standard, the holy thing ultimately the only comfortable thing and the saint the only hero? Are town halls and banks or temples to be the chief objects of architectural magnificence? Is quantity of produce and therefore of profit to be the mark of national greatness or is their fame for good quality and loveliness to be the chief pride of a nation?

Whatever may be the answer which we ourselves would give to such questions, there can be no doubt as to what answers were given by the world which we name as coming to birth about the year 1500. Who shall rule? The rich shall rule and, to that end, the power of kings shall be minimised. What ideas shall be paramount? The idea that national greatness shall be measured by enormity of possessions; that the law shall favour ownership and ownership carry with it no obligation of service; that all men shall bow before money and that those who lend money without risk shall be most highly rewarded for they have loved least. That the responsibility of the common people has no basis in fact; the workman is therefore a tool in the hand of his master. And, as to art, the paramount idea shall be that the workman works for the profit of his employer and not for the good of the work; that the only works which are to be regarded as good in themselves are those works of painting and sculpture, poetry and music which minister to the enjoyment of the rich and those who have leisure. The artist shall no longer be a collaborator with God creating or so fancy himself. He shall be a critic of creation. He shall no longer make things, but only pictures of things and, first of all, pictures of what rich patrons fancy and painted as such patrons fancy them.

The idea of art shall no longer embrace all making; for the responsibility of workmen in general is to be denied and derided except in the moral sphere. The obedience of men to masters, the obligation of the wage-earner to do, in return for his wages, precisely what he is told and to leave all intellectual responsibility and initiative to the owners of the means of production, shall release the workman from any necessity of being an artist. And the artist, that is to say the painter of pictures, the sculptor, the musician and the poet, shall be released from the necessity of making anything useful.

But of course all these answers can be and are camouflaged. The "white man's burden" shall be blown out to hide the profits of colonisation and the exploitation of "backward" nations. The destruction of feudal ideas as to the obligations incumbent upon owners of property shall be shown to be an enlightened departure from barbarism Usury shall be called banking, and kings as well as poor men shall be ruined; thus bankers shall appear to be the saviours of the people. The diminution and denial of the workman's responsibility as a workman is shown to be a good; for the quantitative increase of trading and manufacture for profit which the workman's privation of freedom enables his master to develop, enables the workman to have more boots, more razor-blades, more police, more bicycles, more public baths and wash-houses, more sand-blast patterns on public-house windows, more education and more books. And art, now spelt Art, and meaning only the fine arts (the arts of painting, sculpture, music and poetry), being freed from the shackles of ecclesiastical patronage and the no longer operative rules and regulations of medieval guilds, shall be able to explore "the beauties of nature," and the delightfulness of verisimilitude. From the point of view of the patron, who is now the rich merchant and banker and no longer the church (that is to say the common people; for church art is necessarily popular art seeing that the common people pay for it and look at it), this is a good thing. The artist is exalted by acquaintance with the rich and becomes a gentleman himself, and art, for the first time talked about, shall appear to be for the first time encouraged. It shall come to be thought that art has always depended upon the patronage of the rich and that therefore until the rich became rulers there could be no patronage of art.

But of course all these ideas are not immediately operative, still less immediately acknowledged and stated. It is not until the death of Charles I that the true nature of post-medieval policy is outwardly visible. It is not until the Enclosure Acts that the old peasantry is decisively beaten, the farm labourer enthralled and workers set free for factory employment. It is not until the reign of William and Mary that the Bank of England obtains control of the issue of currency. It is not until the installation of power-driven machinery is made possible by the inventions of James Watt and his colla-borators, inventions which no one would have considered admirable had not a quantitative standard come to be the accepted one, that the factory system of production

breaks the economic resistance of the independent craftsman and the small workshop.

But two things were immediately operative and immediately obvious—the "Reformation" in religion and
the "Renaissance" in art. The Reformation was established by act of Parliament when, in 1534, the act of
Royal Supremacy was passed. The consequences were
immediately obvious; though it was not until the
eighteenth century that it ceased to be necessary to
hang, draw and quarter men and women for religion.
By the end of the eighteenth century the new mentality
was too firmly established to meet with further opposition
or to fear it.

The Renaissance in art was immediately obvious in
painting and sculpture and building. In painting and
sculpture the idea that the basis of art was vision and
not imagination was immediately acceptable. Such an
idea was connatural to the unimaginative; for men of
business, whatever other good qualities they may claim
—such as honesty and forgetfulness of self in the service
of humanity, enterprise and daring in the acquisition of
riches, independence of mind in relation to Canon Law
and the Decalogue—have never claimed to be men of
imagination. They could see themselves in the mirror;
what better could the artist do than hold a mirror up
to nature?

It is true that the representative element in painting
and sculpture had been growing in importance and
popularity for many years before the year 1500 (in Italy
indeed the whole movement was a hundred years earlier),
but it was still subordinate, still not the ruling motive.
After 1500 there was no longer any question about it.

Before the Renaissance painters were like the child who said: "first I think and then I draw my think." After the Renaissance they said: first I look and then I draw my look.*

In the former case the appearance of nature has two grounds of importance. In the first place, the world we live in is the source of all experience. A man could not imagine roundness if he had never seen round things. He could never imagine colour if he had never seen the world around him. He could never imagine the loveliness of arms and legs if he had never lived with and loved men and women. He could never have imagined the clouds and the hills and the flowers and the beasts of the field had he never seen these things, enjoyed them, suffered from them and used them, submitted to them and conquered them. His imagination was filled with them, made of them, nourished and stimulated by them. They were, so to say, the properties of his theatre, the stuff of his trade, the epices of his gaming board. But his imagination transformed them. His imagination was not

* The model for the pre-Renaissance painter was the work of his contemporaries. Plagiarism was unknown because there was nothing else. Our "modern" painter, on the contrary, must at all costs be "original." As the modern engineer studies modern engineering, so the pre-Renaissance painter studied contemporary painting. But, to-day, if Mr. B. copies Mr. A., all the critics condemn him. The reason for this is that, whereas the engineer and the pre-Renaissance painter think and thought of themselves as makers of *things* (e.g. bridges or images of the Madonna), are therefore concerned to make the best possible bridges or Madonnas, and have therefore no scruple about copying (provided that the thing copied is the best and most suitable for their purpose), the modern painter is not a maker of *things* but of self revelations (i.e. pictures of things.) Therefore if he copies other people's work he is a sort of swindler. Before the Renaissance you bought, say, a Madonna. To-day you buy, say, a Cezanne or an Orpen—or even a Lutyens. But in engineering you still buy bridges and not specimens of the work of such and such an engineer.

a camera recording accurately every appearance; it was a sort of kitchen wherein the food for his mind was prepared, re-created, created anew. Art was indeed re-creation.

And the business of painting was the business of getting somehow translated into paint what was seen in the mind—somehow but not anyhow. The act of imagination and the art of painting reacted on one another. To imagine a thing is not necessarily to imagine a painted picture. To make a painting a painting must be imagined. It must be paint from the beginning. It must be of the nature of paint and not paint only by accident. It must be a thing of the imagination and a thing imagined in paint. So also is it with things of stone. So also is it with all other things.

In the second place the world we live in was, for the painter, a sort of dictionary. It was a thing to be referred to when necessary and the degree of necessity for such reference varies inversely with the health and strength of the artistic imagination. If you *know* how you like a woman's arms to go, if you *know* what you love about elbows and toe-nails and rose leaves and tigers, and rocks and smiles and anger and jam, what need is there to go again to look at them and make sketches of them? Nevertheless life is full of such things and they are always available for reference. The only mistake from the point of view of the pre-sixteenth-century artist would be to forget love and remember only appearance.

But from the other point of view, the point of view of what we call the modern world, the world after 1500, it was precisely appearance which was of primary importance. First I look then I draw my look, and the whole art school tradition is founded upon it. The setting up of the model, the landscape, the "still life," the study of anatomy and perspective, light and shade, these things now come first. It is the imagination which is now the accident. The child's drawing, full of imagination, a creature of the imagination, is derided. The child is told to look at things, to observe, to copy things set up before it. Ninety-nine children out of a hundred have neither the patience nor the inclination nor the talent for this production of mimicry, this making things "like" things; so ninety-nine children go into business and the hundredth receives their applause. For though all children begin with the life of the mind, the world of the imagination, their elders, the men of business and their wives and all respectable aunts and uncles, soon knock the "nonsense" out of them and soon, even before they reach adolescence, they are as respectable as their relations and preceptors and as ready to deride the imagination as any one could wish. The whole mind and enthusiasm of the Renaissance, backed as it was from the beginning by all the wealth and influence of bankers and men of commerce, led up inevitably and by a superb march of triumph to the nineteenth-century photograph. The photograph was its great achievement, its pinnacle of accomplishment, its grand anticlimax.

The Renaissance started hampered by the remains of medieval imagination, medieval religion and morals, medieval philosophy. But such things were thrown off one by one; the remains are now only the dregs. It started with the grand idea of man as lord of creation; therefore the study for man is man. It ended with the grand idea of man as a meaningless speck of dust living his little life as the victim of cosmic irrationality, and the artist simply a colour photographer or at best an illustrator of anecdotes.*

I am not forgetting all the great names of the Italian painters and I am not decrying their works; but I am remembering what the books on art have always omitted and what art-critics have always made a point of forgetting. I am remembering the idea of art as it now exists among us. I am remembering the horde of ordinary practitioners. I am remembering the picture shops in the Strand and the one under the Ritz Hotel. I am remembering the pictures in the houses of all my reader's friends and relations. I am remembering the art schools founded after the great exhibition in 1851 to enable manufacturers to recover an elegance which factory articles were beginning to lack. I am not thinking of art as an affair of the Catacombs—catacombs mostly situated on the left bank of the Seine. I am not thinking of modern art as a thing practised and patronised by a small select coterie of highly cultured gentlemen but as the thing met with in ordinary dentists' waiting-rooms and ordinary suburban sitting-rooms. Good or bad, modern art is of a certain kind. Good or bad medieval art was of another kind altogether.

And in the business of building the Renaissance was immediately obvious. It may be difficult to say who

* When I say that the unintelligent buyer of portraits has no other view of the matter than that of a photographer, I do not mean to imply that the intelligent painter has no concern for anything but paint. The portrait painter is a painter; but he is a painter of portraits. Both things concern him. And the buyer of painted portraits is not buying only a portrait; he is also buying a painting. Both things concern him also.

first started digging about in ancient Rome and who first
hit on the bright idea of building imitation Roman
temples. It may be difficult to say when these things
occurred; but, whoever it was and whenever he did it,
the idea caught on immediately and spread rapidly
everywhere. Nor is it difficult to understand this.
Surely it is clear that the medieval house, as at Haddon,
was incompatible with the mentality of the empire
builders. Chatsworth is necessarily their home. There,
within a few miles of one another, you may see the two
minds. Whatever crimes were committed within its
walls, Haddon is a holy house. Whatever the virtue and
largesse of its dukes, Chatsworth is the house of pride,
ostentation, human aggrandisement and worldly success.
Haddon is the house of the builder; Chatsworth is the
house of the architect. The builder builds the only way
he can. His employer must respect this fact or not employ him at all. The employer must share the builder's
enthusiasm. And it is the same with all the different
crafts which house building entails. The mason and the
plumber, the carpenter and the smith, none of these
can, in the medieval world, do other than work according
to his traditions, the living, growing and eventually
dying traditions of his trade. The employer must respect
these traditions also.

Haddon is the house of the builder. There is science
in it as well as love-making. It is a work of construction,
of arches which really span openings and vaulted roofs
which are as much works of engineering as of architecture. It is a work of masonry and carpenter's work.
But Chatsworth had to be designed by a gentleman in an
office, a gentleman who had travelled abroad and knew

how Nero had lived in his prime. The builder had nothing to do with the design of it. He was only a contractor who supplied men and materials. Chatsworth is an architect's house. It has pillars and porticos which do nothing but support architectural fancies and prop up the self-esteem of owners of property. The picture painter of the Renaissance painted their faces; it was the architect's job to portray their civilisation.

Obviously the medieval tradition of building was dead by the year 1500. That tradition had thriven in a quite different atmosphere. It grew in an atmosphere of war between princes, tempered and sometimes even curbed by the peace of Christian faith and morals. It died in an atmosphere of commercial excitement, the growing power of merchants accompanying and in harmony with the corruption of the church.

The merchant princes of the late Middle Ages did their best to coerce medieval builders to build houses suitable to their pride. Churches and town halls also suffered from their subscriptions and became more and more redolent of the prevailing atmosphere. Endless repetitions of cuspings and panellings showed the riches of the benefactor and the waning inspiration of the builder. There was a certain sobriety and solemnity about some or many of the houses and churches of the fifteenth century but it was the sobriety of the unimaginative merchant and the solemnity of the workman who was no longer gay.

By the sixteenth century the medieval tradition of building was dead. It was as dead as feudalism. It was as dead as medieval philosophy and morals. Painting and sculpture were in the same plight. The trade in

English alabaster carvings was only redeemed from the gross commercialism of the nineteenth-century church furniture shop by the fact that, in the absence of modern machinery, the work had perforce to be done by real men. In music, the chant of the church like the architecture of the period was overlaid with meaningless ornaments. In spite of much charm, as in the Market Cross at Chichester, and much real grandeur, as at King's College, Cambridge, it was a period of decay.

It was in this atmosphere that the new world came to birth and it was a congenial atmosphere. The Reformation and Renaissance were, as is commonly the case in the affairs of men, entirely misnamed. There was no reforming of ideas nor any new birth of art. The proper word is Fulfilment. The sixteenth century saw the fulfilment of humanism. It was one movement not two. The discords were merely temporary or merely apparent. The great lords of the Renaissance certainly did not appear to be moved by zeal in religion. The genius of Luther and Calvin and Cranmer and Knox did not outwardly show any connection with the resuscitated grandeurs of ancient Rome or the luxury of the papal courts. Nevertheless the world was one world. The artistic ideals of the architects and painters, the sculptors and poets and musicians, were dependent upon the breaking down of the barriers to freedom of thought and freedom of trade. But, the barriers being removed, the modern world was free to develop according to its own nature, to produce works not so much meet for repentance as meet for pride. Though the holy was necessarily denied to us, for the holy is in some way superhuman and stinks of paradise, nevertheless the good was still possible and

good works have been produced in abundance. There
have been good works of all kinds throughout the whole
four centuries. What need is there to catalogue them?
We must note, however, that the great works of the
period have all been works of secular importance. It was
a secular inspiration which produced St. Paul's Cathedral
and all Wren's churches as it was a secular inspiration
which the Jesuits exploited on the Continent and in
South America.* The architecture of the Renaissance,
the Fulfilment, had a secular inspiration. It conformed
all the time to man's fine idea of himself. It was an
architecture first and foremost of grand exteriors. No
longer was the exterior, as in the caes of the medieval
cathedral and the medieval house, simply the necessary
result of the interior. The builder, that is to say, if you
wish, the architect, was no longer concerned, as the first
reason of his existence, to put a covering over an altar
or over a hearth. His job now was to put up an imposing
monument, a thing to be seen by the passer by more
even than by the enterer in. The church and the mansion
became different kinds of mausoleum. Necessarily there
were interiors and, often, as at St. Paul's Cathedral in
London and at St. Sulpice in Paris, very grand interiors
indeed. But the exterior was the thing of primary importance and, if necessary, the interior was sacrificed to it.
Windows were placed where they most suited the architect's notions of exterior composition. Roofs not con-

---

* That indeed was the special genius of the Society of Jesus: that
it took the modern world without criticism. The society was born in
the modern world and knew no other. Its mission was to save souls
by instruction and preaching. It had no ambition, as the Benedictines
had in the wreckage of the sixth century, to plant, so to say, a garden
suitable for christian men to live in here below.

sidered seemly were hidden by parapets. A false dome was put on St. Paul's because the real one would not have been sufficiently tall and imposing when seen from the street, and the buttresses were screened from prurient gaze, as though they were a sort of indecency, by high walls decorated with imitation windows.

Architecture became a grand game of play-acting and the audience walked about the streets and enjoyed the performance. The interiors of churches became less important the less people went into them. There is no doubt that people go to church less than they did and church accommodation which, in the Middle Ages, was greater than the population, is now not sufficient for a tenth of us. Grand mansions and banks are not places for the entertainment of common men, naturally, therefore, common men are satisfied if they are outwardly imposing. And outwardly imposing they were, especially in the early years of our world. It was a sort of springtime. Trade and piracy were flourishing. The new world of America was offering adventure to the bold and profit to their backers. The new worlds in the sky discovered by astronomers showed the falsity of the old ecclesiastical theories or seemed to do so, and a great weight of authority in faith and morals was lifted off financiers' minds. If the church was wrong about astronomy, there seemed every hope that she was wrong about usury.

The time was full of a new enthusiasm, and this was inevitably reflected in the arts. Moreover the architects had two great advantages in those early days, advantages which as years went on they were to lose. In the first place their new-found enthusiasm for the buildings and ornament of ancient Rome was, just because it was new-found, a thing without precedent. You could not say to a young designer: you must not do such and such, it is not done. There was no respectable rule which all respectable people followed. Everything was fresh; all works were experimental.

And in the second place architects had the advantage of being able to employ workmen who still retained some of the responsibility of the workmen of the preceding centuries. Division of labour, labour-saving machinery, labour-displacing machinery such as was developed later, were still non-existent. The workman was becoming enslaved but he was still a human being, he was still, at the worst, only a slave in the manner of the slaves of ancient Rome. He might be tied by the ankle, he might suffer every economic disaster, but he must still use his hands and his head. They had not yet arrived at the stage wherein the mouldings are cut by machine planes and all that the workman has to do is to trim the ends of the stones which the machine necessarily leaves ragged. The machine still served the workman; the workman did not yet serve the machine. These two things: the experimental nature of the work of the architect and the humane nature of the work of the workman lent a freshness and liveliness to the work done which we in these later days cannot rival or approach. You have only to look at the common cottages of the early Renaissance to see these things. Architecturally they are free from all that business which modern schools of architecture have been at such pains to inculcate. Though they imagined themselves to be building in the style of ancient Rome they were really making a style of their own. Their knowledge and scholarship were puerile compared with what the schools have since accomplished. The architects were amateurs and their works were amateurish. Tudor and Jacobean attempts at classicism were childlike and naive. The architect had not yet systematised his knowledge, the contractor had not yet regimented his men. Quaintness happened without being aimed at; in the nineteenth century they had consciously to aim at it if they were foolish enough to want it and to think you could get it by aiming.

The same enthusiasm inspired the arts of music and poetry. It is not that the Elizabethan poets or the music of Bird and Palestrina are to be thought of as propaganda for a secular idea. It is rather that poetry and music ceased to be propagandist for the religious idea—at least by intention. The individual poet, the individual musician, emerges as an artist known by name, just as the individual architect and painter and sculptor were emerging. The thing now called "fine art," differentiated from the general business of making, now emerges as an occupation suitable for educated gentlemen. Your architect, your painter, your musician, your poet escape from the ranks of builders and decorators, and from the yoke of church service, and become the specially favoured friends of the rich bankers of Florence or London. "Art patronage" emerges. And this patronage is necessarily the patronage of the newly emancipated merchant and banking class, a class no longer subordinate to princes of church or state, but dominant, a ruling class, lords of the new world.

The quality of this patronage is immediately evident in the works of the artists patronised. It is a predominantly secular patronage and could be no other. Portrait painting, hitherto scarcely known, comes immediately to the front. Before this time the idea of paying a painter to paint your portrait or even that of your wife and daughters was abhorrent. The idea clashed with the spirit of medieval civilisation. Such works of portraiture as were done were not portraits at all in the modern sense of the word. They were rather of the nature of symbolic representations. The king's figure on a coin represented kingship rather than the physiognomy of this or that particular king. Down to the time of Elizabeth there was no attempt on the part of the artist and no demand on the part of the customer for anything but a generalisation. Sculptured effigies of barons and bishops were what we call conventional rather than naturalistic. And the conventional is not that which is made according to an arbitrary code of the unnatural but is, as the word implies, an agreement in matters of natural behaviour or the representation of the natural. There is nothing unnatural about a convention. It is not a departure from nature but an agreement as to the true nature of the natural. What, for instance, we call a conventional rose is not a rose drawn in a way contrary to the nature of roses, but, on the contrary, it is a rose drawn according to what we all agree to be the nature of roses in general. On the other hand what we call the naturalistic is not an attempt to express general truths about things but to express the truth about particular things, and that is why the business of portrait painting received such a tremendous ovation from the newly enfranchised princes of commerce. They saw themselves as men of power. They wielded a power they themselves had won. It was not a power conferred upon them by the agreement of peoples or by divine or supposedly divine authority, but one resulting from their own prowess as manipulators of trade and commerce to their own personal advantage. The great baron of the Middle Ages was, even in his own idea of himself, a vassal. The great bishop was, to himself and to his flock, a servant of servants. If he betrayed his people he was known as a betrayer and hated as a betrayer. But the new princes of commerce owed no such allegiances and suffered no such condemnations. They made their money and owed service to no one, and they had their portraits painted.

Naturally the fashion spread. Kings saw themselves and were, by their new masters, encouraged to see themselves as fine specimens of humanity. Man discovered himself, especially rich man, and poor man stood by and admired. What else could he do? In good time the poor also would see themselves; but the photograph had not yet come.

The portrait is the symbol of all the arts of the Renaissance. And in the course of time the painter came to conceive of the whole business of painting as the business of portraiture—portraiture of himself. His paintings were more like him than they were like anything else. If he painted a landscape it was a painting of the landscape as seen by him and was, therefore, a revelation more of himself than of the landscape. What he thought and what he left were the things that mattered most. The tables were now turned. The painter who, in the Middle Ages, had been the servant of an idea, an idea shared by the whole population and who had become, in the Renaissance, the servant of a patron, now, in the end, became his own master. Art became, and was proclaimed to be, the expression of emotion, the artist's emotion, his self-revelation. The work of art became simply an object for the machinations of picture dealers, dealers in things whose value lay in their peculiar rarity.

The nineteenth century saw the peak of this strange metamorphosis. As much as two hundred thousand pounds was paid by infatuated persons for what they called an "old master." And this happened not once or twice but frequently and as a matter of course, and was thought of as a right way of spending public funds and a natural way of encouraging art

In the early days of this art-dealing the technique of criticism was of course undeveloped and any person who possessed what he could plausibly claim to be the work of a "master" labelled the thing "attributed to so and so." Thus in the course of time the public picture galleries and private collections of Europe and America were filled with works of whose authorship there was no certainty. But, in this business, certainty of authorship is the main source of value. If only one could be certain one had a painting by Raphael Sanzio then, instead of a beggarly fifty pounds, one could get perhaps a hundred thousand from the sale of it. Naturally it followed that anyone who could prove or disprove the authentiticy of paintings was a person of great importance. The science of "art criticism" developed on these lines. Certain persons appeared who had a peculiar genius for the business. By precise examination and comparison of different paintings they were able to bring irrefutable evidence to prove authorship or disprove it. The result of this process was that, out of perhaps a thousand paintings

c

"attributed" to Raphael, only ten were found to be authentic. The remaining nine hundred and ninety were condemned henceforth to be labelled merely "school of." A thousand paintings valued at fifty pounds each became ten at a hundred thousand and nine hundred and ninety at a hundred shillings. It does not take much calculation to see that the gain to the dealers was enormous. Some of them became extremely rich and were made lords and barons.

But in spite of this apotheosis of the artist and especially of the "old master," princes of commerce, wealthy men of business, the chief patrons of art in this modern world, still regarded the painter and sculptor as persons whose real business was to flatter them. The portrait still held the chief place in their esteem. To be a fashionable portrait painter was to have reached the highest pinnacle of honour, and to paint things suitable for the "drawing-room" came to be the thing specially called "art."

I insist on this way of looking at it because it is a way which is commonly avoided. It is vital. By our division of the world of making into working men and artists, by our degradation of ordinary labour to the level of the ant-heap and by our setting apart of painters and sculptors as a specially expensive kind of workmen whose works can only be acquired by the rich, we have done a wholly abnormal and monstrous thing.

There is another point of view. The secular inspiration, the profane genius of the "Renaissance" is not without its own special grandeurs. Things have been done and things made which could not otherwise have been done or made. Could the "Bacchus and Ariadne" of Titian have been painted under any other auspices? Could the Baroque churches and castles of Germany have been built? Could Shakespeare have written *The Tempest* or Beethoven the Sonatas and Symphonies? Could Keats have existed or Coleridge, Browning or Meredith, Manet, Whistler or Cezanne? The contribution of these men and of the thousands who have, so to say, collaborated with them, though it be a contribution to the world's treasure which the millions of industrial proletarians and their masters can never appreciate because it is neither of them nor for them, is a spiritual contribution so great as to make all the other activities of modern man seem worthless. In the light of such things it seems as though all the other things should be subordinated, all other ambitions and enthusiasms spurned and that to these artists all other men should be sacrificed.

But the flattery of the rich is, notwithstanding, the real origin of their works and though beside the flattery, woven into it, transcending it, exalting and obliterating it, is the disinterested enthusiasm of spiritual beings— man, matter and spirit, inseparably both—nevertheless art is more than "fine" art and man is more than men. The productions of these modern artists owe much of their importance to the fact that the work of all other men has been reduced to inhuman dullness or imbecility. The productions of individual genius and sensibility do not, even in their own line of business, reach such heights as the productions of communities labouring under the inspiration of ideas communally accepted and communally loved.

It is therefore altogether outside my scheme to describe the technical developments and æsthetic theories of the last four hundred years. That has already been done by people better qualified to do it. Art is more than fine art, more than æsthetics, more than the business of producing psychophysical states. It is more than the adventures of specialists in self-revelation however intimate and moving. Art is the business of making in general. All things made are works of art—that is the theme of this book.

* * *

The change which led to the peculiar segregation of the artist from the mass of ordinary workmen was of course a gradual one. Kings and princes did not immediately surrender their thrones and have even now not been obliged to surrender their crowns. It is doubtful whether Elizabeth knew that the Cecils were the real governors of England; it is certain the people at large did not know it. Architects and painters had no suspicion (at least, none is recorded) that they had exchanged the status of workman for that of lapdog. Make a man a knight and a fellow of the Royal Society and it is difficult for him or his fellows to believe that he is not a greater man than the anonymous architects of previous ages. The new world was ruled from the city instead of the citadel, from the bank instead of the bishop's bench, but the results were not immediately apparent; the theocratic traditions of centuries could not be immediately discarded. It is only in a general view such as this book attempts to spy out that we see the secular inspiration clearly permeating the whole world. Individual works and individual artists were still moved by the older ideas, and few individual works or individual artists are even yet entirely free from them.

Meanwhile in the arts not called "fine" there was no radical change of method or ideas. Furniture makers, metal workers, weavers still carried on according to the traditional methods. The new style in architecture made only a superficial change in the shapes of tables and chairs. You may recognise a Jacobean chair directly you see one, but as a piece of carpenter's work it is not radically different from its predecessor. Carpentering, bricklaying, smithing was still the work of responsible carpenters, bricklayers and smiths. England was still an agricultural country, growing all its own food. Foreign trade was still only the exchange of surplus goods. No country thought of itself and certainly England did not think of itself as a country living by the exchange of manufactures for food. Such a state of affairs could not be brought about in a country in which most of the farmers were still peasant proprietors. Nor was such a state of affairs even hoped for by the new secular lords. It was no part of their scheme to set up a manufacturing country instead of a self-supporting agricultural one. They were concerned for their own aggrandisement, and the dispossession of the peasantry was seen only as means to that end.

But whereas the presence of a self-sufficient peasantry was abhorrent to the landlords, a mass of unemployed and property-less labourers was, so to say, "jam" to the manufacturers. Turned off the land, men flocked to the towns. The supply of cheap and unorganised labour made the factory system possible. The thing grew unregarded. So far as it was noticed it seemed admirable. Unemployed men found employment. Things were multiplied, trade increased, fortunes were built up,

banking flourished. Our governors saw themselves as
the righteous man who is never forsaken and as the
good man who is never to be seen begging his bread.

But for the most part the thing was unregarded. It
was not a portent; it was seen as the natural and inevitable development of "enlightened" government. And
the factory system grew quite independently of the
invention of machinery. There was no machinery in the
early factory. The factory was simply a large workshop
in which division of labour was the only novel economy.
But water and steam power were being experimented
with. By the middle of the eighteenth century the steam
engine was a practical affair. It only needed the discovery and exploitation of coal to make it the universal
engine of commercial production.

For the accumulations of capital which had been made
possible by the exploitation of dispossessed human
labour were as nothing compared with the accumulations
discovered in the earth. It is difficult for us, a hundred
and fifty years afterwards, to imagine the fever of the
Industrial Revolution, the almost sudden enlargement
of men's powers, an enlargement entirely unprecedented.
For thousands of years, in spite of varying climates and
varying political circumstances, men had made things
with the unaided power of their hands. Tools such as
the wheel and the lever were understood but power
other than hand power was hardly known. Water power
was undeveloped; almost the only helper was the horse.
Armies still marched in the eighteenth century as they
had done in the time of Alexander. Julius Cæsar's march
over the Alps was still the fastest known. The sawing of
stone was still done by hand. Bricks and even nails

were made one by one. Now suddenly we were able to harness the sun to draw the cart. We had had to live by human labour; now we could call in the inhuman force of Nature. We had lived on income; now we could live on capital—an apparently inexhaustible hoard. Before 1750 there was not a fire but somebody had grown the wood. After 1750 we could burn the wood grown and accumulated thousands of years before human history began. The opportunity was not lost upon the manufacturers. The peasantry was finally defeated by the Enclosure Acts. Ireland, Scotland, even the Continent of Europe could be recruited for cheap labour. The idea of England as the workshop of the world emerged into consciousness. We'd got the coal, we'd got the men, we'd got the money too. And no one else was doing it. We could flood any country with our cheap factory productions. No one could compete with us. It was the business man's paradise.

We need not consider here any other aspect of the affair but that of its effects upon the thing called art. Its political effects, the rise and spread of trades' unions, the fight for new markets throughout the world, the colonial expansion and the white man's burden of spreading British culture in all countries capable of being exploited, these things are outside the scope of this book.*

But, like the Reformation and the Renaissance, the Industrial Revolution was misnamed. Like them it was a fulfilment, an inevitable development, a flowering of the plant. Consciously or unconsciously Protestantism

---

* Nor need we consider the grandeur of the powers which Industrialism has conferred upon us. Engineering and applied science have received and will receive their due reward without my assistance. I do not decry these things or deny them.

was unreal. Consciously or unconsciously the Renaissance was unreal. Humanism was unreal. The real thing was Commercialism. Things had always been bought and sold, but now that was their first reason for existence. The buyer still wanted hair-brushes for his hair, boots for his feet, churches and town halls for meeting-places; but that was no longer why they were made. They were now made simply as merchandise. To the simple-minded consumer there seems to be no difference. The village blacksmith had been a man who made ironwork for him. The Birmingham factory has ironwork to sell. What is the difference? The difference in the kind and quality of the ironwork was not immediately noticeable. By the time that it was noticeable the buyer had become too accustomed to the change to notice it. But the difference in the point of view of the person who supplies the goods is obvious. Blacksmiths meet one another as fellow workmen. Iron-masters meet as men of business. Blacksmiths meet in the village "pub." Iron-masters meet in the Chamber of Commerce. However avaricious he be, a blacksmith is a workman who makes things of iron. However true it be that an iron-master supplies iron goods, he is chiefly a man whose business is making money. A printer is a man who prints books; he may be a bad man, a liar and a thief. A master printer is a man who makes money by selling printing; he may be a kind husband, a good father and a pillar of the Established Church or of the Society of Friends.

These two points of view will of course overlap. The smith must get money for his horseshoes; the iron-master must supply iron in return for your money. But the mechanism is different. The smith's place of business is his workshop; the iron-master's workshop is his place of business—the workshop in the one case, the office in the other. The test is whether you do business with a man in his workshop or in his office. Of course there is every sort of variety and things shade off into one another; but the principle remains clear. A man of business is different from a craftsman. He is a special kind of craftsman; his craft is buying and selling; the only thing he is concerned to make is money. Craftsmen too are interested in money—the necessities of the family compel it. And many men of business are interested in the things manufactured in their factories—they are compelled to be so by the rivalry of other factory owners; you cannot sell your goods unless you can claim for them that they are in some way superior to other people's. The difference remains obvious. Making is different from selling. The growth of the factory system made the man of business everywhere victorious. The idea, the ideology of business achieved its fulfilment with the Reformation and Renaissance but, in the absence of cheap dispossessed labour and in the absence of anything but the power of human muscle, business lacked its fulfilment in material expression. While things must still be made one by one and by hand there's very little money in it—unless, of course, you can hold them up, "corner" them, obtain a monopoly in them; but your fellow merchants will do their best to stop this, and with a fine air of public spirit, obtain legislation against you. In such a world scarcity is the business man's friend. But now, with cheap labour and machinery, the supply of things in quantity became, for the first time since the decay of Rome, the means to riches.

C*

Buying and selling had been the chief enthusiasm of our rulers for two and a half centuries but there had been comparatively little to buy and sell. Now power was multiplied a hundred or a thousandfold.

The old craftsman attitude of mind was incompatible with the new way of manufacture and the old craftsman was generally incapable of mercantile enthusiasm. The conduct of manufacture fell into the hands of a different class of men, a higher class, a class having literary education, a black-coated class, a roundhead class, a class which, as it admitted no intermediary between itself and God, admitted no intermediary between itself and money-making.

What was the effect on things made? Apart altogether from the question of good or bad, better or worse there is the difference of kind. The factory article is a different kind of thing from the things made one by one by a man who, at any moment, to suit the requirements of a particular customer or his own sense of fitness, may change their shape or quality. The factory workman is a different kind of workman from his predecessor and he works in an entirely different way, with a different frame of mind; it is inevitable that the things produced should be different.

Nevertheless, as in the first days of printing the printing types were as close imitations as possible to the handwriting which preceded them (for letters are letters and A is A whether you write it by hand or dent it in by metal type), so in the first years of factory production every attempt was made to produce things which looked the same as the things made before. And this was by no means a matter of commercial deceit even if, as some hold, commercial deceit had been the motive of the first printers. A is A whether written or printed, and tables and chairs and all other things are like letters in this respect. They are an accepted convention. A chair for the parlour is recognised as being a certain kind of chair, different from a kitchen chair, different from an office stool. It is not only different in architectural shape, it is different in the kind of decoration which is applied to it. Decoration is what is decorous. The trappings of the drawing-room are indecorous in the kitchen. So a factory-made chair had to conform to the conventions. If it differed in workmanship it did not differ by definition. Factory owners and factory workmen were still filled with pre-factory notions of things. It was to take more than a hundred years to educate either the manufacturer or his customer to the proper notion of the nature of factory products, to get them to see that pre-industrial conventions had been arrived at by the exchange of ideas between men who wanted things and men who made them; whereas industrialism is a process in which men who want and men who make never meet and all negotiation is between the managing directors of the factory and the commercial travellers whose business it is to find out from shopkeepers what will sell. This absence of intercourse between makers and users necessarily means that the thing made is no longer a thing made by one person for another. The personal business is now ruled out of the transaction. You no longer go to a shop and buy what is made in that shop by the person who runs it, though of course there are still survivals here and there of this pre-industrial way of doing business, survivals, it is curious to note, chiefly supported by those who have made money through the industrial system. Few wealthy owners of clothing factories will dress in "reach me down" suits of clothes made in their own factories. They prefer to imitate the habits of the surviving nobility and gentry and have their clothes specially made for them by their "own" tailors. But in general the shops have now ceased to be workshops and shop assistants are only the salesmen of things made elsewhere.

And as the personal business is ruled out between maker and user, so it is between the maker and the work. Things are no longer made as the user orders, nor even are they made as the workman chooses. A workman's choice can only be operative when he is a person actually working for persons and when he is a responsible workman working in control of all the relevant processes of his trade. In a factory neither of these conditions is present. You neither deal with the customer, the consumer, nor control the process.

The implications are now obvious; but they were not obvious in 1750 or even in 1850. And this was not entirely a matter of stupidity on the part of either producer or consumer. It was neither commercial deceit nor stupidity which caused the standard and conventions of a hand-working world to prevail for a century after the introduction of machinery. These standards and conventions prevailed for so long because the introduction of machinery and the breeding of intellectually more or less subhuman mechanics was a slow process. Not everything was immediately machine-made; not every workman immediately became a mere tool, a tooth on a wheel. Even now many processes in manufacture are still hand processes. Moulding machines in the stone trade still leave ragged ends for the mason to square up with mallet and chisel as in the time of the Romans or the Plantagenets. Routing machines still fail to get into corners and so make work for a mere man with a mere knife. And if this is so to-day, it was much more so in 1800. In many trades power-driven machines were not used at all for several generations and in those trades where machinery was used it was at first only used for preliminary stages of manufacture. The idea of using a machine to make a thing from start to finish, including the packing, did not exist, had not arrived. Consequently the idea of the thing to be made was not the idea of a machine-made thing. It was the idea of the old hand-made thing, made more quickly and in larger quantities, and therefore at greater profit, with the assistance of machinery.

But if the introduction of machinery did not immediately change the conventional ideas of things to be made, the government of manufacture by men of business instead of by tradesmen, that is men trained in the trade, did, wherever such government was effective, mean the immediate destruction of the essence of the thing called art. The idea of the artist is "formative of things and not formed by them."* The form and the content are inseparable. A chair imagined by an artist is a chair imagined as made—down to the last possible detail of material and workmanship. He cannot see a chair except as a thing of material, this material or that, made in this way or some other way. Before the introduction of machinery all chairs were works of art because they

* Maritain, *Frontiers of Poetry*, p. 89, English trans.

were all the product of imagination directly operative upon material. This is true even of the early factories in which, though no power-driven machinery was used, labour saving was effected by division of labour. For in such places, however much the workmen were driven by their own poverty and by "grasping and avaricious men," the things made were necessarily the product of human labour. The workman still needed both will and intelligence, and even if a man was only responsible for a chair leg and no longer for a whole chair, the leg was itself and by itself a work of art, a thing made by a workman who was, so far, responsible. His idea of a chair leg was a formative idea, an idea formative of things and not formed by them. But the introduction of machinery, wherever it was introduced and in so far as it was introduced, did immediately destroy the responsibility of the workman and therefore his power as an artist.

This fact is a consequence of the historical ownership of machinery and is nothing to do with the nature of machinery itself. It is perfectly possible to make good things by machinery. It is perfectly possible to make works of art in a proper sense of the word. But to bring this about it is necessary that the machines shall be owned and controlled by the designers of the things to be made. That is the thing which the historical introduction and ownership of machinery has not allowed. Machinery was not introduced by the workman in order that a different kind of thing, a machine-made thing, might be made. It was introduced by men of business solely that money might be made and for no other reason whatever. And machinery has up to now remained in the control of men of business. While that is so it is only by accident, or the peculiarity of a disinterested or intelligent man of business (such a person is necessarily peculiar for a man of business is by definition not disinterested and has no more need of intellect than a wasp) that machine-made things are either good to look at or good to use.

It was perhaps inevitable that the history of machinery should be what it has been. It is difficult if not impossible to imagine any other chain of circumstances than those which actually occurred which could lead up to such an accumulation of capital as was necessary to make the invention and construction of machinery possible.* Moreover it must be remembered, and this is a point generally forgotten by those whose minds are suffused by the delights of wireless telegraphy and the many other conveniences and services of commercial enterprise and of the commercial application of the results of experimental science, that the accumulation of capital was not in itself enough. It was necessary also that there should be an accumulation of unemployed labourers, proletarians, to work the machinery introduced. For though the prime reason of machinery from the point of view of those who actually introduced it, the men of business, was, as it still is, the saving of human labour, it was not, in the first days of the Industrial Revolution, that is to say the Commercial Fulfil-

---

* "The Protestant Reformation, for example, is far more a political than a religious event, and cannot be understood apart from the struggle of the rising bourgeoisie against the confiements of Feudalism. The Catholic Church in the sixteenth century was not only incomparably the greatest of landowners, but was the ideological backbone of the feudal system, nationally and internationally. In England especially, the plunder of the Church played a big part in that primitive accumulation of capital without which the modern industrial world could never have come into existence." (*New English Weekly*, Jan. 4, 1934, p. 285.)

ment, introduced to save the labour then clamouring
for employment. On the contrary it was to use that
labour, to exploit it to the utmost. The purpose of
machinery was to save the labour which would have
been required to make the vast quantities of things for
which they envisaged markets and which, in the absence
of machinery, would have been altogether too costly to
produce. That supply of labour was available. It had
been made available by the landlordism which succeeded feudalism. What the avarice of merchants did
not supply was supplied by the avarice of the new
landed gentry.

Whatever we may think of machinery in itself and as
an agent for the production of things desired, we must
remember its twofold origin—the growth of capitalism
and the dispossession of the peasantry. Machinery, as
has frequently been said, was not invented to make
things better or even to help the workman. It was not
introduced either by the workman or the designer of
things to be made. Its origins were neither humanitarian
nor artistic, but purely commercial.

But machines in themselves have always been works
of art. The designers of machines have never entirely
rid themselves of their humanity or been able to refrain
from regarding their inventions as beings to be contemplated as ends. To the engineer as to the toolsmith, the
machine like the tool is worth making for its own sake.
A good saw may be nothing more by definition than one
which will cut well, but its makers have never regarded
it so simply. A good locomotive may by definition be
nothing more than one which does the work demanded
of it, but neither its designers nor its users have ever

yet seen it thus. On the other hand the workman, except when he saw his employment jeopardised, has always been willing to think of machines as tools and has welcomed them as implements to do away with the more laborious kinds of work. The perspicacious consumer may see virtue in the variety of surface shown in hand-sawn floorboards and adzed roof timbers, yet, though introduced for the sake of his master's gain, the circular saw has received no condemnation from his employees.

But it is with reference to the things made that the question of machinery is chiefly of importance here. And it is precisely the things made which have been machinery's main failure. They have been failures for the simple reason that no man of business can afford to be disinterested. Men of business are necessarily at the mercy of the undisciplined fancies of those who buy things and the undisciplined desire for money of those who advance the capital. Between the capitalist and the consumer the man of business is between the devil and the deepest part of the Atlantic Ocean. The growth and multiplication of joint-stock companies has developed in the investor a frame of mind morally indistinguishable from that of the usurer pure and simple. The spread of machine industry on commercial lines and competition between rival manufacturers has brought it about that the buyer's fancy is the only test commercially applicable. And the buyer being, in the majority of cases, himself either a factory hand or a clerk in the business has no standards by which to judge the good quality of anything.

From its first beginning the use of machinery has been exploited simply as a profit-making instrument. Up to the end of the nineteenth century there could not be said to exist any good machine-made things except the machines themselves. In fact no one had up to that time so much as thought of the word "machine-made" as meaning anything but a machine-made version of what would otherwise have to be made by hand. The only factory articles which could claim to be as good as hand-made were things which without machinery could not have come into existence. You may safely say that a fountain-pen or a typewriter is as good as they could be made by hand because they could not be made by hand at all. They could not be made, because they could not be made cheap enough if you had to make them one by one or by simple division of labour. Apart from such things, all that the factory system, up to the end of the century, had given us was a vast output of more or less cheap and always bad imitations of what had, before machinery, been better done by hand.

What a triumph! Space had been conquered. The locomotive and the steamship had made it possible to travel with safety in a few hours or a few days to places it had formerly taken weeks, months or years to reach. But by a progressive degradation and cheapening of everything made, a degradation which spread as far as railway or steamship could penetrate, this conquest of space was turned to ashes. Every foreign culture was reduced to our level. In the end the natives of India, than whom no people could claim a greater refinement or more venerable civilisation, were happy to buy from Lancashire cheap imitations of their own woven fabrics, and it was a matter of great profit to the money lords that the heathens of Africa should use inferior brass idols manufactured in Birmingham. The white man's burden was carried on his own soul.

But this degradation was not noticed by the majority of our people. Perhaps that could hardly be expected. The habits of mind derived from the practice of thousands, perhaps millions of years could not be discarded in a mere hundred. Buildings, clothes, furniture, food and drink had been the customary vehicles for man's artistic exuberance since the beginning of his history. Man is a tool-using animal and "the tool is from the beginning that of the artist no less than that of the labourer."* That things were for delight as much as for use and that usefulness and delightfulness were inseparable are ideas connatural to him. It was perhaps not to be expected that he would see immediately that shapes suitable for things made by the old personal methods of manufacture were naturally unsuitable for things made by machinery. It was natural that designers of machines should think it their business to design machines which would make things of the same shapes as heretofore and to ornament them as they had always been ornamented. Moreover, men of commerce have never been innovators. New ways of making money are the only things for which they can claim any originality and, even in that, the city is inclined to be timid and dull and the same old ways of cheating are still the most popular. What has been sold before can be sold again. Certainly it was not to be expected that manufacturers and shopkeepers and their backers, the bankers, would either wish for or promote the making of anything except imitations of what they and their customers were used to.

* Christopher Dawson, *Progress and Religion*, p. 72.

So the second half of the eighteenth century and all the nineteenth saw the orgy of romanticism. "Things are not what they seem," sang the poet of the period. Nor, we might add, are they what they pretend to be. Nothing could be more pretentious, that is to say more false and romantic, than for example the buildings of what is called the Gothic Revival. The style of building called "Gothic" was first and foremost a technique, a kind of engineering in stone, a method of construction evolved specially for a material which would stand crushing but not bending. But Gothic was more than that, though that was indeed its first principle. It was the enthusiasm of whole populations, just as wireless telegraphy is to-day and cricket was yesterday. It was the vehicle for the expression of their whole mentality. It was a mystical and holy thing as much as an adventure in practical building. In the Middle Ages every building was a Gothic building, the castle no less than the cathedral, the cottage no less than the palace. There was no other way of building though in no two years and at no two places was it ever the same. It was not a style of building chosen because rich people liked it or because they thought it suitable for churches. It wasn't chosen at all. It grew, flowered and decayed like the natural thing it was.

But Gothic in the nineteenth century was an adventure of architects and sentimental ecclesiastics. The medievalism favoured by men of business, who love to think of themselves as burghers and councillors (moreover to be a councillor is to have a finger in the control of municipal spending), was another contributory cause of it. The town halls of Manchester and Bradford are notable examples of this romanticism, this hypocrisy, this civic buffoonery. If nineteenth-century architects had taken up Gothic simply as a reasonable technique for building in stone (assuming that building in stone was at that time a reasonable thing to do) and had pursued the method in a spirit of rationality, as the medieval builders did, at the same time acknowledging the difference between the type of labour employed and the consequent necessity for eschewing all ornament, the Gothic Revival might have been a venerable phenomenon. With the increased powers of mechanical knowledge and mechanical appliances they would have been able to put up buildings of unexampled architectural magnificence. As it was, the whole adventure and all its enthusiasm were frittered away in medievalism, an attempt to reproduce the appearance of a past age. Luther had declared that the human intellect was incapable of arriving at truth. His followers believed him. The architecture of the nineteenth century was a consequence of this intellectual suicide. Men no longer believed in the validity of human reason. Architects and their clients wallowed in make-believe. The art of building became a branch of the art of the theatre, play-acting, the business of putting up façades having no reasonable relation to the business of construction. There are only two essential qualities necessary to be pursued by builders—good construction and holiness. Good construction depends upon the integrity of the intellect; holiness upon moral integrity. The architects had surrendered the one; their clients had no use for the latter. Nineteenth-century buildings dressed up to look like buildings of the thirteenth were the produce of imbecility on the part of architects and of hypocrisy on the part of their clients.

And what is to be said of nineteenth-century Gothic applies equally to nineteenth-century imitation Roman or Greek. It was all sham, all deceit.* Colonnades and porticoes and pediments were not real colonnades and real porticoes or pediments. They were things put up in front of the real buildings of iron and brick—the real buildings of which both architects and their clients were ashamed. Colonnades and pediments copied from Greek and Roman temples did not really represent the dignity of civic life in the nineteenth century; for that civic life had no real dignity to represent. There is no real dignity in buying and selling. The market booth of poles and canvas is their proper and decent housing. In such a panoply chaffering wears appropriate weeds and may affect an appropriate gaiety, but the architecture of temples and palaces is preposterous and misleading.

I do not attribute any moral fault to anybody; for, apart from the strict injunction to "judge not," it is manifestly impossible to judge justly (no one knows his own motives for certain, still less other people's), and though it is incredible, business men themselves believe that they are simply the victims of blind economic forces and have neither control over nor responsibility for their business dealings.

I do not accuse any individual of fraud. It was the

---

* Perhaps a footnote is sufficient to answer the possible criticism that my attitude is the typically British one of the moralist. The difficulty is in the words "sham" and "deceit." If I call nineteenth-century Gothic a sham and its architects deceivers, I appear to be accusing them of sin. That is not my intention although there is such a thing as culpable ignorance. My appeal is to reason. I say such things are silly. I say, as Nietzsche said, "it is worse than a crime, it's a folly." My indignation is not so much a product of moral rectitude as of intellectual exasperation.

fashion of the age. It is hard for a rich man to enter the kingdom of heaven; still harder is it for him to build the heavenly Jerusalem. He can but build what pleases him and what can possibly please those whose enthusiasm is the power that comes from riches but a sort of ornate vulgarity? How can he care for holiness whose whole life is spent in getting the better of his neighbours or his rivals in trade at home or abroad? How can he care for integrity of construction whose whole life is concerned with the manufacture of what will sell, whether good or bad? Yet it is not the fault of men of business that they are such and not otherwise. A man of business is by definition one engaged in trading and the business of trading is buying and selling, buying cheap and selling dear, selling at the largest possible profit, whether by a large profit on a single transaction or a million small profits on a million small ones—that is business itself. The fault does not lie with the man of business; he acts according to nature. The fault lies in his insubordination. He is a servant, we have made him king. He is a servant, we have made him high priest.

If nineteenth-century architecture was play-acting, so also were nineteenth-century poetry and painting and sculpture. But architecture is a public art and one depending for its existence upon the collaboration of many men working together, so that it may be said that even the smallest cottage is the product of a whole civilisation. Poetry and painting and sculpture, on the contrary, are arts that can be pursued in private. The make-believe of the poet is his own private affair. He will not sell his poems unless what he writes arouses a response in those who read; but his needs are compara-

tively small. He can write a decent poem on twopenny-
worth of bad paper; he does not need to call in a contractor or borrow hundreds or thousands of pounds from
a bank. So also, in less degree, the painter and sculptor
can pursue their callings without much expense. To be
successful from a middle-class or bourgeois point of view,
a "worldly" point of view, does of course involve these
private artists in the same kind of flattery of rich men
as is incumbent upon the architect; but if they choose
to remain in their attics they may do so and still pursue
their private fancies.

The nineteenth century saw the growth of private art.
As public art, the arts of architecture and architectural
sculpture and wall painting, became more and more completely submerged in commercial aggrandisement, so
private art, driven into its attics and cellars (places
called studios, in Chelsea and Montparnasse—Parnassos
—the abode of the gods!) became more and more private
and idiosyncratic. It was play-acting; it had no relation,
except as a reflexion and a criticism, with reality, with
the real life of industrial cities and commercial prince-
doms. "Back to nature," cried the artists and it was the
most romantic cry of all—as though things were not
everywhere proceeding according to nature all the time,
as though factory chimneys were not as natural as blades
of grass! Is a factory chimney supernatural? Is it a
miracle? Are machines the work of either angels or
demons? Are houses unnatural in London but not unnatural in country villages? What they meant when they
cried "back to nature" was back to fancy, back to fairy-
land, back to the only reality Luther had bequeathed to
the modern world—the reality of their own emotions.

Salvation is by faith he had said; and the only faith remaining to the private artists of the nineteenth century was faith in themselves.

Curiously enough this development was quite satisfactory to the men of business. Poetry did not affect them one way or another; though if the poet applauded their enterprises they were quite happy to honour him. But architectural sculpture, so far as they could see, could be quite adequately executed by hired mechanicians working from full-size drawings supplied by the architect, and as for paintings, they could be bought separately and hung up in frames if you wanted them. But, except for portraits of lord mayors and directors, there was no real need of paintings; for paintings do not show from the street. Magnificence outside, comfort within, these are the two requirements of those who pay for commercial architecture.

Nevertheless private art was not by any means without patronage from merchants and financiers. A painting properly authenticated, done by a man decently dead so that no more works can come from him to reduce the scarcity value of those he did before he died, done by a man for whom the dealers and art critics have been able to build up a reputation, done in a manner not too revolting to the morals of Oliver Cromwell and not too blatantly subvervise of business stability—such a painting is both a good investment and a mark of superiority. To have the right paintings on your walls is nearly as important as to have the right number of buttons on your waistcoat—more important indeed; for whereas you cannot advertise your good taste in buttons, you can bequeath your paintings to a public gallery and earn the undying respect of a grateful nation. Knighthoods and even peerages have been won for less.

Nineteenth-century architecture was necessarily almost wholly bad. It was too much entangled in publicity and the attempt to put up humane appearances with the aid of subhuman "hands." But the private artists, from their dim and tragic cells, brought forth works which, though exotic and redolent of the hothouse, represent a remarkable series of adventurers in the cultivation of artificial flowers. So remarkable have been these adventures, these excursions into secret and often forbidden pastures, that in many minds, and almost in popular speech, the name of art is now exclusively reserved for them.

But in any case the private arts of the nineteenth century are a side turning and a blind alley. However poignant, they are always introspective. The artist, deprived of public service, turned upon himself, dug into his own vitals, probed his own sensations. The man of science dissected matter in the hope of discovering the truth; philosophers pulled truth to pieces in the hope of discovering good; and artists tore open their own souls in the hope of finding beauty. Forlorn hopes! The reward of science has been its application to money-making. The reward of philosophy has been its acceptance by the politicians. The reward of art has been its enclosure in a glass case.

This history of the private arts of the nineteenth century is a matter for special essays. How Bauedelaire succeeded Wordsworth and converted the Wordsworthian study of man's reactions to sunsets into a study of man's

reactions to his own state of nerves.* How the business
of the story-teller became less and less a recreation of
things seen and things done and became more and more
a reproduction of things felt by the writer—a revelation
of psychology. For, as the work of the world became
more mechanical, the lives of the people became stereo-
typed and, under police supervision, sterilised. The only
things remaining worth writing about were the interior
mental adventures of the few remaining unsterilised
people, interlarded with descriptions of the few places
remaining unmechanised. The factory has seldom been
the subject of paintings and factory life seldom extolled.
Factory chimneys look fine against sunsets, and giant
cranes are fine things in themselves; but these things
were unknown to the nineteenth-century romantics. A
book might be written to show how the historical paintings of Delacroix foreran the anecdotage of Luke Fildes.
How the colour photography of royal academicians and
salons produced the reaction of the impressionists and
that, in its turn, the reaction of Cezanne. How all these
"movements" were attempts to discover reality in a
world which, for three hundred and more years, had
proclaimed reality to be undiscoverable by the human
mind. How during all this time men of commerce were
carrying on regardless, or merely exploiting these movements. How money-making itself became an art, and
millionaires, living on barley water and biscuits, eschewed
even power over their fellows, and rejoiced like war
horses to scent Wall Street from afar. These might be
the titles of as many separate monographs. And another
monograph might be written to deal solely with the

* See Appendix 2.

development of æsthetics. Many such already exist. They are the natural result of the nineteenth century's great achievement in divorcing the idea of work from the idea of responsibility and the idea of art from the idea of utility.

"Architecture,' said Walt Whitman, "is what you do to a building when you look at it." Architecture! that is to say beautiful building. Beautiful! that is to say building which pleases when seen. But the building is no longer of importance to the poet. The poet's only concern is with his own emotions. The first duty of every man is that most completely selfish one of saving his own soul. But that duty no longer involves first of all the love of God and your neighbour, it now only involves, first and last, the duty of complete self-satisfaction. I feel therefore I am.

Such, in outline, is the history of the Fulfilment. Reformation, Renaissance, grand words signifying neither reform nor rebirth, and Industrialism, the true word at last, not industry, hard work and application to duty, but Industrialism, that is to say, in the moral sphere, the exploitation of the labourer for the aggrandisement of his master, the control of production for profit instead of for use, all things regarded as merchandise, and the reduction of the workman to a subhuman condition of intellectual irresponsibility, and, in the sphere of art, the idea that all necessary work is a necessary evil to be relegated to the sphere of the drains! Buildings, furniture, clothes and food are still called "goods" in the account books of men of business, but they have ceased to be goods in the account given of them by those who make them. They are merely the source of wages, wages for the procuring of necessary evils.

It is possible to conceive an Industrialism which is not commercial in its directorate. Such apparently is the Industrialism conceived by the Marxians in Russia. Such is that conceived, we are asked to suppose, by Mussolini and those who support him. Under such a régime it would be possible, it is at least imaginable, that directors of work, designers of things to be made and of the machines to make them, and the machine minders and transport workers would all be moved by a common and even holy spirit of mutual service and esteem. "There is a war on," say the Russians, "let us behave as patriots." But, however patriotically directed, Industrialism, though robbed of its moral evil, would still depend upon machine industry, and machine industry, in spite of the grandeur and beauty of machine-made things properly designed *ad hoc*, would still involve the condition in which the only fully responsible workman would be the designer and all the rest of the workers would, as regards their work, be no more than obedient tools, ants rather than men. And if the time come when machines have been so perfected as to need no human guidance or supervision, or at most only a few hours by a few men per day, even so Industrialism would still mean that necessary things, houses, furniture, clothes and food, things which during all the centuries of man's history have been his chief means for pleasing himself, his only means for collaborating with God in creating, would be deprived of that beauty which is the special mark of human work, the beauty of tenderness and sensibility in the actual handling of material things.

Let it go, they may say; plenty in a world of machines is more important than tenderness in a world of scarcity. Moreover, they will add, there will be plenty of time for tenderness in the long leisure of a morally perfected industrialism. In that long leisure the private arts will flourish.

CHAPTER IV

Art in the Twentieth Century

BRIGHTON is due south of London, yet you cannot get there by walking due south all the time; there are too many brick walls in the way. The nineteenth century was the last period of the commercial Fulfilment; but the course of true commerce never yet ran smooth and it is likely that its final decline will be no more clearly visible to us than its rise was clearly visible to the Elizabethans. Generalisations are always absurd; yet they must continually be attempted. Though we live from moment to moment we must plan at least a few months ahead. The general view from my window may be different from the view obtained by anyone else. My window may be higher or lower than yours, the glass more translucent or less. Nevertheless there is a general view possible and I must do my best to describe it. I must do my best to see through the brick walls and do my best to weed out from my predilections and prejudices those which are only foibles and personal fancies.

The modern world (but it will soon cease to be "modern" and a new name will have to be found for it) is the world of the commercial fulfilment. In that world the man of business first emerged as ruler and the world of things first became for its rulers a world of nothing but merchandise. In the nineteenth century the modern world began its decline and the twentieth century will see the end of commercial rule. This must necessarily

95

be so; commercialism is even now in the agony of death and rattling in its abominable throat. Commercialism is not the rule of the machine though machinery was naturally beloved by men of business and fostered by them. Commercialism is simply the rule of the trader, the buyer and seller; its mortal disease has been brought about by its own rapacity. By making money its god it has placed itself in the power of those who use money as a thing to be bought and sold. The banker, the gombeen man, the money-lender, is the death of all who bow to him.*

The history of art in the commercial period has been the history of the art of salesmanship. Step by step things have been sacrificed to entries in account books. "To goods" in the merchant's book means anything or nothing; the only entry that matters is in the money columns. Use has been sacrificed to profits. And the degradation of things was necessarily brought about by the degradation of the workman. The first step in that process was the degradation of kings and princes— those who stood between men and merchants.† The

* In Jerusalem to-day the money-lenders call themselves bankers. Would that, in London, the bankers had the honesty to call themselves money-lenders!

† The reader need not point out to me the countless well-known examples of tyrannical princes, dishonest and rapacious kings and corrupt courts. Nor need he point out the superior sanitation enjoyed by modern London and New York, the fact that physical torture is now seldom used in courts of justice or that the modern workman has higher wages and whiter bread. In this book I am not concerned to discuss degrees of physical comfort or suburban refinement. I am only concerned with the changes which have occurred in the style and quality of things made. The reader may prefer the rule of money to that of kings; but he must no longer deny that merchants, being under the domination of money-lenders (i.e. bankers and investors), are more interested in good profits than in good things.

next was the dispossession of the peasantry. The last was their enslavement in the factory.

Now the problem of art in the twentieth century is: how to arrange or organise the state so that the making of things shall be controlled by those who make them and those who use them and removed from the control of those who merely sell them. The problem for those who are concerned for the good quality of things made (and that is the same as saying the problem confronting everybody) is the problem how to break the commercial spirit which now moves everyone, whether in big business or small, whether in high places or low, and how to break the power of international finance in time to avert a series of wars more disastrous than the last and thereafter the complete collapse of civilisation in the west.

The solution of this problem is not the business of this book. It is only necessary to state it here because the problem of art, the making of things, is not an academic problem concerning no one but the professors of art schools and exponents of the private arts; it concerns all the makers of all the necessaries of human life. Is it reasonable to assume that a solution will be achieved? Or must we suppose that the international financiers and all the millions of small business men, for whom the "orthodox" economy has now displaced the Protestant Bible as a sacred and infallible teacher and guide, will be able to resist the break-up of their power until, like Gadarene swine, they hurl themselves into destruction? Let us follow this unsavoury line and assume that the death-bed scene of commercialism will last till the end of the century. The twentieth century will be the stage

D

upon which will be played out the drama, tragic or comic, of the struggle of naked man, as it were Laocoon, with the twin snakes of Usury and War. What will be the history of art during that struggle?

Let us survey the stage set for the drama. Art is the business of making things. In the minds of those who control the business of making things, things are primarily merchandise, things to be bought and sold at a profit. That is the point of view of the controllers; it must not for a moment be forgotten. It is the controlling factor, and all other ideas are subordinated to that one. The enthusiasms of engineers, of builders, of furniture designers, of the makers of golf sticks and of those who play with them, of painters and poets, sculptors, musicians and writers of books, of dressmakers and cooks, of scientists, philosophers, preachers and priests, are enthusiasms waging more or less successful or unsuccessful war against the enthusiasm of makers of money. Money rules; under that rule art must do the best it can.* The business of the merchant is buying and selling. Buying leads to selling; the successful salesman is the successful merchant. But what will sell? This depends upon the nature of the customer, man. Man is a creature who, from the point of view of the merchant and many of his scientific supporters, like all the other animals has no

---

* "I have not seen the righteous forsaken nor his seed begging bread" (Psalms of David). This is the scriptural basis for commercialism (our civilisation is based upon it), and in the absence of authority as to the nature of righteousness, judgment must depend upon profits. If your business prospers you may count yourself righteous. In confirmation of this I may quote the words of a leading man of business. Proposing a vote of thanks at the close of a lecture on art he said: "The man of business who does not think only of profit but gives due attention to good quality will find at the end of the year, when he faces his accountant, that he has not served his God at a loss."

free will or power of deliberation. Man, the consumer, eats and drinks what is set before him. He can do no other. The person who can go out of the whole caboodle and eat and drink such things as he can grow and prepare for himself is an eccentric, there are not enough of him to count. Man, the consumer, is a herd. What will the herd buy? The herd will buy what by mass suggestion, advertisement, publicity, can be made to seem what he *must* buy. The consumer is full of vanity—appeal to his vanity. He is a snob—get him that way. He is hungry and thirsty—tell him at every street corner and every hundred yards along every main road that *Lirvob* will make him strong and that *Sennisug* is good for him, and he won't be able to stop consuming the things. Tell him he prefers a *Sabb*, tell him often enough, and he won't be able to deny it. He is extremely "hard up," that is to say his wages are never quite enough to buy all the things he and his fellow workmen and the masters between them have made (and under the present financial system the disproportion tends to become greater and greater), tell him that if he buys a hundred packets of your cigarettes you will give him a new gramophone for nothing and he will buy your cigarettes like a bird— so will his wife and daughters; no power on earth can stop them. Tell him you will give him twenty shillings for fifteen shillings and ninepence—he won't know how you do it but he will believe you and will hand over his fifteen and nine like the petty usurer you have made him. But, and here the marvellous thing called "enlightened self-interest" comes in, it is just as easy to make him buy good things as bad, if you advertise the right way, and, strange as it may seem, all things work together for good. The object of the human intellect, whether we believe in psychological determinism or not, is the truth, and whether or no we believe in free will, the object of the will is the good. It is therefore inevitable that truth will prevail in the long, long run, and though "bad money drives out good," good things have, even now, a small advantage over bad ones. A mass-produced cast-iron lamp-post decorated to look like the work of Benvenuto Cellini comes in the course of time to be distasteful even to London County Councillors. "Period" furniture, in spite of its immense snobbish appeal to those who, though they live in Wimbledon, have seen through the glass in Wardour Street and South Kensington Museum, is a sham and therefore eventually abhorrent even to the owners of golf sticks. And plain things made by machinery can, by good advertisement in plain language, evoke a quite genuine response from creatures for whom furniture is, after all, a thing to be used. The appeal of utility is on the whole a safer appeal and "better business" than the appeal to "good taste."

And, in architecture, the factory is winning. In some ways it is really a blessing that orthodox economy keeps everyone short of money. God knows what an orgy of impossible architecture men of business might not now be imposing upon us were it not for the fact that they are all now more or less bankrupt! As it is they have been forced to give attention to economy and economy is the most salutary principle in practical æsthetics. There is now no chance of another St. Pancras Hotel being built. The building of the Prudential Assurance is now seen to be extremely improvident. The galaxy of "star turns" presented by Oxford Street, in which each shop endeavours to outshine its neighbour in mercantile magnificence, now makes a lantern slide at which all young architects laugh. The Bank of England could not of course emulate the intelligence of the *Daily Express*, moreover the bank is a kind of temple and must wear the garb of respectable sanctity (have we not now bank holidays instead of the holy days imposed upon us by merely ecclesiastical authority?) but, in general, there is a marked tendency for buildings to become decently plain. The front, the thing seen from the street, is still of course subject to old-fashioned architectural magnificence; but even here mouldings and sculptures are, by the mercy of God, departing. There are, at last, a few really good architects and a few who are really putting up buildings. There are a few architects who have really escaped from the play-acting obsession of the period of the commercial Fulfilment, men who actually see building for what it primarily is: the covering of a space and for whom, therefore, the interior is not an accident. Such is the irony of the situation that they have to call themselves "interior architects"; but they are the only real architects we have had since the Middle Ages.

In fact the engineer is emerging as architect. The man of constructional intelligence is ousting the sentimental designer of façades. And, in the factory, the man who studies the machine and the nature of machinery including the nature of the "hand" and the nature of the subhuman, is ousting the student of museum specimens of pre-industrial hand work. Furniture, pottery, utensils, textiles are now to be obtained, not

only plain and unornamented but of a shape suitable
for mechanical production. The business of making
reproductions can now only claim a right to existence in
the sphere of the private arts, the arts which, in the
nature of things, the factory cannot originate.

You can make things by machinery; but you cannot
express emotion in them. You can jangle people's
nerves in a power house; but you have no power to say
what it feels like. Factory articles are the product of the
consciousness of the herd; they are not the product of
the self-consciousness of any individual. You can put up
factory buildings alongside the mountains; but it needs
a painter or a sculptor to appreciate and record his
appreciation of the relations of their masses. You can
make all sorts of noises; but you cannot write a tune
by machinery, still less an orchestral symphony. For
paintings and sculptures and music, for poems, detective
stories and psychological novels, you need the individual
mind controlling the individual hand and responding to
the individual eye or ear.

But you can have reproductions of paintings and
sculptures and music just as you can have, if you will
be so kind, ten thousand copies of this book. You can
have reproductions of drawings and paintings such that
if you put them side by side with the originals you, and
not even museum curators, would know which was
which. You can have gramophone records as near as no
matter like a band in your boudoir. Thus the makers
of such things will grow rich and art will be spread
among the multitude. Four thousand, nay, forty millions
shall be fed with a few loaves and fishes. How much
better that all the inhabitants of Burslem and White-

chapel should have facsimiles of Van Gogh's yellow old chair than original photographs by the local photographer! And thus art, now meaning "fine" art, the art of fine feelings, far from being destroyed, as was feared, by Industrialism, is to be given a new lease of life. As the novelist hopes to be a best seller (and the publisher hopes so too) so the painter and musician hope to see reproductions of their works in every English home.

Architectural sculpture and painting are dead—you can't properly do carvings and paintings on machine-made walls, any more than you can do repoussé work on iron girders, and this truth will be out before long—but there is still the sculpture of the niche and the pedestal, the former a kind of glorified town-crier proclaiming in silence the name and purpose of the building. (Prudence for the Prudential; St. Pancras for the L.M.S.) the latter a sort of violin solo in stone performed in the place where a bandstand might be. And there is still the painting of the frame; no, not necessarily gilt, for, though you and I will probably have reproductions, someone will have the original if it is not in the National Gallery.

And Church music is dead (let's be honest—do musicians go to church, does anybody? I mean how many could if they wanted to?) and street cries are forbidden (for the klaxon forbids competition) but the concert hall must be preserved if only for the sake of the radio—sans fil et sans reproche.

So while on the one hand we see the bulk of the population in these early years of the twentieth century firmly entrenched or encaged in the life of the factory, and as far as their own work goes, deprived of any possibility of self-expression, the expression of their own fine feelings, the thing now specially called Art and honoured as such; on the other hand we see the veritable apotheosis of the "artist." Far from being a down-trodden member of society, he is a god. Even financiers worship him. And though there is no noticeable increase in the numbers of unemployed factory hands who visit the National and municipal picture galleries, we are informed by the highest authority that among members of "the working class" there is a real demand for the best music on the "wireless" when they are not working.

On the one hand we have the recognition of the beauty of the machine and the beauty of the true machine pro-duct, the thing made as machines alone can make it, the thing devoid of any extraneous, irrelevant, sentimental pseudo-humane quality. On the other we have the recognition of the value of purely useless, non-didactic, non-anecdotal, non-representational painting—the deco-ration purely as such and in itself and not as being the decoration of or on anything. The patronage which was given, in the early days of the commercial Fulfilment, to the art of making paintings which were, when pinned up, like holes in the wall through which you saw into a room or a landscape other than what you saw by looking through a door or out of the window, is now given to the art of making paintings which are, as it were, peep holes into the bare soul of the painter. The business of holding a mirror up to nature now means holding a mirror up to the nature of the artist. It means nature subjectively felt and not nature objectively seen or imagined. How-ever many vulgar people there be who still love pic-tures to be like holes in the wall, such pictures now have no more prestige than the fat carved legs of their owners' billiard tables.

On the one hand we have the artist concerned solely to express himself; on the other is the workman deprived of any self to express.

The majority of the working class are not artists in any sense of the word; they are neither responsible workmen nor purveyors of emotions. If they were not spenders of their own wages they would be better doped and put on shelves when they are not at work. That is the horrid dilemma confronting our politicians—the paid representatives of our men of business—that the more machinery is used the less men are used, and the less men are used the fewer people there are with effective purchasing power. Men must buy or merchants must weep. . . . National credit! No, that is crankiness—as disastrous and as cranky as the idea of loans without interest—nothing so indecent can be discussed here. Here we are concerned simply with the fact that we have developed a civilisation in which the majority of those who make things or assist in making them are neither responsible for the quality, the serviceable quality of what they produce nor for the production of anything expressive of themselves. On the other hand a minority of workmen, the people quite rightly called artists, both those who are designers of factory articles to be made by machinery and those who are designers of paintings to be made with their own hands, are fully responsible for what they make. The things they make are the rproduct of their own skill and are the expression of their own minds.

And as their responsibilities are different (in the one case the purely moral responsibility of slaves, in the

D*

other the full responsibility of freemen), so are their works. On the one hand are all the "useful" things, the necessaries of life, on the other are the useless things, the things for entertainment. For though the designer of factory articles is the designer of useful things it is not as such that he is employed. Useful things could be made and were made without him. He is employed to give an entertaining quality to things otherwise dull and unsaleable. From the point of view of his employer he is the same kind of artist as the person who exhibits his wares in those places of entertainment called art galleries. He is the same in kind; he is only more meritoriously, because more profitably engaged.

And, as useful things become more and more purely useful, the artist designer of them finds the greatest difficulty in curbing the enthusiasm of commercial travellers for the ornate and fanciful (commercial travellers, like bishops, won't take any risks, moreover you can camouflage a lot of bad construction with ornament). And, as entertaining things become more and more purely entertaining, the painter of paintings has to curb the enthusiasm of art dealers and common men for the useful picture, the picture *of* something, the picture which tells a story, the picture with a meaning.

But things of use are rapidly becoming more purely useful, things of entertainment more purely entertaining and delightful things more purely spiritual. Art which in the tenth century was never mentioned is in the twentieth century the one thing worth talking about.

The peculiar achievement of the nineteenth century in separating, in thought and in fact, the idea of work from the idea of art, the activity of the "workman" from the activity of the "artist," has made the subject of art of general interest whereas, before the Industrial Revolution, it was only of interest to specialists, and, before the Renaissance, it was of interest to no one.

Art embraces all making—all things made are works of art. But, in the twentieth century, the word art only means the "fine" arts, the arts which are concerned with the making of those things which minister to mental satisfactions alone, whereas art in the general sense ministers to satisfactions both mental and physical. In the twentieth century the dilemma is becoming both obvious and tragic. On the one hand is seen the gradual emergence of the "useful object" shorn of all "art-nonsense," all factitious allurement or ornament or caprice, the true product of the machine—beautiful because truly functional, therefore satisfactory to the mind, therefore pleasing when seen—and at the same time the degradation of the workman from the position of a responsible craftsman to a subhuman condition of intellectual irresponsibility, with the consequent necessity of providing for his amusement and culture by means of state-controlled and state-censored cultural and educational organisations. On the other hand is seen the extraordinary development of the fine arts now that they are freed from their age-old entanglement with physical utility, and the extraordinary position of the "artist" who, though he is responsible to no one but himself, is the only responsible workman left—he is the only workman whose power of choice is effective in the work of his hands.

On the one hand the twentieth century will witness the worship of human personality and sensibility in the arts of poetry, music, painting and sculpture; on the other will be seen the complete suppression of personality in the common workman as such—he will only be human in his "spare time," the time when he is not working.

CHAPTER V

Tools and Machines

IT might be urged, why all this to-do? Why not let the whole thing "rip" as heretofore? Why not let the styles of art take care of themselves? Why bother to do by reason what the process of time and man's natural tendency to the true and the good will do in any case? Messrs. Maple & Company's over-ornamented furniture has inevitably become distasteful to the best people. Nineteenth-century architecture is falling before the reasonable building of the twentieth. The ornamental is everywhere giving place to the plain.

These views leave out two considerations of great importance. In the first place: it is not true of human works that they are, like the dam of the beaver, the product of the blind instinct of animals. Man's works are primarily the product of his ideas and of his imagination. Influences which have borne upon his mind have always changed the kind and quality of his works. It is indeed impossible to say at any point: here is the product of reason untouched by instinct; for man is an instinctive animal as well as a rational soul, and in any particular work reason and instinct impinge upon one another and the work is a product of both; moreover man's consciousness is underlaid by his subconscious and acts which are not consciously reasoned are not necessarily simply instinctive. But to say that there is no need to appeal to reason, that things will right themselves without any

109

such appeal, is precisely the doctrine which in four centuries of Protestantism has brought us to the present mess.

In the second place it is not possible to "let things rip" because the processes of production which Industrialism has introduced are not in the direct line of descent from those which preceded them. We have introduced a radical change. The introduction of machinery is not, as some would fondly believe, simply the introduction of more elaborate and costly tools. The machine age is not simply man producing more quickly and more easily, with less physical labour and with less burdensome toil and in greater quantity what he had hitherto produced by hand without machinery. So to state it is to state it wrongly.

For there is no longer any need to deceive ourselves. Machinery is not the same as tools. Machinery is not used either to help the workman or to make his work better. Nor was it introduced for humanitarian reasons. Stokers on steamships would still be shovelling coal, as stokers on locomotives still do, it if were not more economical, that is to say more profitable, to employ other methods. Machinery is used as it was always intended to be used, ever since its first introduction, to save labour. And to save labour means to do away with labour—to make labour unnecessary and therefore to make the payment of wages to labourers unnecessary.

This fact was camouflaged in the early markets—especially the unsaturated foreign markets. The introduction of machinery appeared, in the beginning, to increase employment. That was an illusion. For though they employed many more men than before, they produced a vastly greater quantity of things than could have been produced by the same number of men without machinery, and therefore they saved, that is did not employ, the amount of labour which would have been required to produce that greater amount of things if machinery had not been employed instead of men.

Machinery is not to be confused with tools. You can if you like, call tools machines or machines tools, but you cannot say there is no difference between doing things the way you yourself intend and doing them the way the designer of the machine or tool intends. If I take a piece of iron and with my fingers and various tools (or machines if you prefer the word) shape that iron into the shape of a box, *because that's the kind of man I am*—that is one thing. If I take a similar piece of iron and put it into one end of a machine (or tool if you prefer the word!) and it comes out at the other end a box, *because that's the kind of tool or machine it is*—that is quite another thing.

I shall keep to the old usage and call those things tools whose object is to help the workman to do his work, and I shall call those things machines which require the workman to mind them rather than use them. The former help the workman to make *things*; the latter help his master to make *money*.

Nor must we be led astray by the fact that tools and machines fade into one another. Some tools, as for instance the printer's hand press and the wood-worker's or metal-worker's lathe (with the chisel held in the hand), embody more of the principles of machinery than do simple hammers and chisels. On the other hand, some machines, as for instance the locomotive (whether on road or on rail) and the household sewing-machine, retain more of the nature of tools than do, for instance, the bookbinder's casing-machine or the letter-founder's casting-machine.

The test is always the relation between the work done and the man doing it. If the shape and quality of the things produced are matters for which the workman is responsible, that is one thing; if he is not responsible it is another. The responsible workman uses tools; the irresponsible "hand" uses machines, or, rather, he is used by his master to *mind* machines.

You may say (it has often been said) that man is a tool-using animal. And you may say that the "master" is an animal who uses machines. The printer uses the hand-press; the master uses the power press. All is as it should be. Only let us be clear about it. The question is not whether machines are good or bad, beautiful or ugly; nor whether machine-made things are good or bad, beautiful or ugly. The only questions here are: what are machines and what are they for? And it is particularly important to remember that, however good they are in themselves and however good are the things turned out by machinery, machines used in manufacture were not introduced either for the good of the work to be done or for the good of the workman. Improvement of quality may be worth achieving from the point of view of the workman either for its own sake, or for the sake of prestige, or out of pure swank and "art nonsense"; but from the point of view of the man of business there is only one possible excuse for good quality and that is "good business."

The comfort of the workman is obviously a matter of

importance to himself and there is no reason whatever to suppose that factory workmen have ever resisted the introduction of machinery on any other ground than that it did away with employment. The independent craftsman has not resisted machinery, he has simply rejected it—it did not offer him what he wanted. But it is the "workman," the employee, the proletarian, upon whom and upon whose penury the master depends: and the proletarian has never had any complaint to make against machinery as a way of doing work. On the contrary he has been the first to welcome relief from the drudgery of quantity-production by hand. The production of a daily newspaper with a large circulation in the days of the hand press involved the compositors and pressmen in almost fiendish labour. The spinning and weaving industries of the early factory days and the clothing trades up to the end of the nineteenth century presented spectacles of inhumanity from which the introduction of machinery meant a most blessed release. Nevertheless humanitarianism is not the idea of machinery; if hand-sewn button-holes are cheaper, hand-sewn button-holes they will be, until the police put a stop to it, or until the whole business world goes bankrupt.

The only object of machinery in the manufacturing trades is to do away with employment. Few people want to be employers of labour because an employer is a nice thing to be. If you can buy a machine to mind a machine, you will gladly buy it—provided the costs of production are thereby reduced. Even the bankers who can make money, literally, by a stroke of pen, and destroy it as easily (though they do not allow the fact to be published in the daily press) prefer machine calculators.

That is to say they prefer one calculating-machine to six clerks. "One loves one's men," yes, but not to the extent of preferring them to profits. And even if some men like employing other men, what will the shareholders say if dividends are sacrificed to sentiment or an Alexandrian lust for power? Limited liability does not mean a limited appetite for the largest possible profits.

And just as people talk of unemployment as though they wanted to cure it (while all the time they are taking every opportunity to introduce labour-displacing machinery) and as though they liked being employers more than anything else, so they talk about "craftsmanship." Of course there are still a lot of old-fashioned workmen who, both in mind and by birth, are still imbued with pre-industrial notions of work—old-fashioned stone masons who still talk about "Gothic" and "Gilbert Scott"; old-fashioned printing compositors who still talk about doing a decent job; old-fashioned railwaymen who still call a locomotive a "she"—nevertheless, the craftsman, like his language is only a survival of the Middle Ages. In the really modern printing factory the only real craftsman is the "keyboard operator" and that's a much better name for her; and the only real craftsmanship is "machine-minding" and that's a better name for that

And as they still talk about employment and craftsmanship so they still imitate the appearances of pre-industrial things. Steamship funnels are still "raked aft" (as they say in pre-industrial language) in imitation of the masts of sailing-ships. Tea-cups still have flowers and patterns in imitation of peasant pottery and the pottery of the Chinese. They still put machine-made mouldings on doors in imitation of the work of the eighteenth-century joiners, just as men still wear collars and ties although the collar is now only a kind of necklace and the tie ties up nothing.

The point here is that all these things are not merely developments (as when medieval spires got more and more pointed and higher) nor are they merely natural survivals (like the nipples on men's breasts); these things are now simply anachronisms. By the introduction of machinery into factories not only were the men reduced, in the blessed theological phrase, to "a subhuman condition of intellectual irresponsibility" (the men do not care and nor do their masters) but the work was radically different in kind. It is no longer human work, and therefore excusably redolent of the human personality of the workman; it is machine work and therefore has no right to be anything but redolent of the machine.

Machines can do neither ornament nor the ornamental. If we want ornament we must make it for ourselves in our spare time—the time when we are not "working." That is going to be what spare time is for.

Men formerly made things—even in the slave system of ancient Rome or eighteenth-century America. Now it may truly be said that things are made by machines. Formerly man made as he chose; now he must make as the machine will allow.

Production by machinery has produced the artist who is simply a designer. Every kind of work requires a designer because every kind of thing made is a thing made first of all in the imagination and someone must draw it out. But equally obviously, before industrialism, the business of design was commonly the business of the workman who actually made things. Now the designer is an entirely different person and one who need not actually make anything but a drawing.

But machinery runs according to the laws of mechanics and not according to either morals or æsthetics. Therefore, the more purely mechanical become the functions of the workman and the more purely mechanical his product, so much the more incumbent upon the designer is it to know and observe the laws of mechanics. The designer's imagination must conform to the machine. He must see machine-made things in his head. He must forswear the snobbery of men of business who cling to pre-industrial appearances and are ashamed of the machine-products out of which they make their fortunes. He must see the beauty of machine-made things even if his employers in their radio-fed suburban villas cannot do so. You cannot have it both ways. You cannot have things made by machinery and pretend with success that they are made by human beings. But there need be no lack of beauty. There will be the beauty of Nature herself than which nothing is more truly functional.*

* We may note that though the private artist is becoming more and more the exponent of his psychological reactions, and therefore less and less the purveyor of "utilities," his reactions are conditioned by the industrial world, and it is machines and the shapes of machines, their precise and geometrical forms, which most deeply move many of the most sensitive of modern painters and sculptors. In this respect their work should, one would suppose, make great appeal to industrialist and factory hands, even more than to other people. But it is not so. Your industrialist, whether master or "hand, ' is prone to wallow in sentimentalism and romance. He still prefers Marcus Stone to Bracque or Brancusi and thus "private art," in spite of its dabblings in such matters of public interest as machines, becomes more and more private.

The influence of "fashion" is very strong in these matters—what we might call "collar-and-tieism." It is probable that the inhabitant of Bloomsbury would be horrified if he heard it said of him that he had the morals of a nun and a Carmelite nun would be horrified if she were told that her paintings were "post-impressionist." The scientist who

CHAPTER VI

Invisible Art

ART before the commercial Fulfilment of the sixteenth century was not a subject of conversation; more, it was not a thing anyone thought about. Even the philosophers who, like St. Thomas Aquinas, wrote and thought about everything under the sun, did not write or think about art as a special subject, a thing practised by some people and not by others.

In those times there was no special thing called art. Art was making in general and anyone who made anything would, if the word had existed, have been called an artist. Art was simply the way of men with things; it was human work as opposed to the inhuman productions of Nature. If anyone was called a master of arts it was one who had mastered the humanities; and this may still be seen by the title given to persons who, in those medieval institutions called universities, have passed more or less successfully through a course of

---

applies the utmost acumen to the exact design, and no "art-nonsense," of an electrical instrument will accept without question the suburban manners and the irrational dress of his university, and it will not cross the mind of a professor of Greek philosophy that his pupils ought or could be actually Platonists or Aristotelians in their citizenship of the British Empire. The Army chaplain will condemn the pacifist as a fool and the Red-Cross nurse will pin white feathers in his button-hole. The capitalist will invest with equal enthusiasm in either munition factories (at home or abroad) or in hospitals or in both. To be like everyone else in your particular set or group is everyone's ambition and the man who attempts to see all things in order together is thought to be merely a crank.

117

studies in human language, philosophy or divinity and have eaten a certain number of dinners, or attended at chapel a certain number of times.

And as art, the thing we now call art, was not talked or thought about before the time of Luther or Raphael or the Medicis (those great bankers) neither was it so much as seen. Art was as invisible as it was unheard of. Sculpture as such was invisible. Architecture was invisible. Painting and poetry and music were invisible and inaudible. The sculptures of Chartres were stone carvings in as much as they were made of stone, but they were ordered and paid for as stone kings and queens and saints, and not as objects of æsthetic satisfaction. Doubtless their makers and their makers' patrons got æsthetic satisfaction from them—who could not?—but that anyone could pay for that pleasure and order it from a workman was an idea that did not exist. Beauty looks after herself if you give her the proper conditions. Give a well brought-up child of seven a box of paints and a pencil and paper, there will be no lack of beauty in its productions though it has never heard the word beauty mentioned and has no idea of making anything but people and things of paper and paint.

But to-day the situation is rather different. The preindustrial habit of thinking of things as *things* and letting beauty take care of itself still persists among children and the "working classes"—among the poor there is still no such thing as art for art's sake. But among the rich and among the educated—and these classes do all the writing and talking about it—art is now neither unmentioned nor invisible. And the word now means something quite different. It no longer means *things* or the *making* of things; it now means simply the exhibition of the worker's sensibility and, chiefly, his appreciation of the *relations* of things. It is now commonplace among the intellectuals to say that it does not matter what things are, whether they are useful or otherwise, appropriate or inappropriate: all that matters is the relations between them. The visual relations between a top hat and a mug of Guinness placed on a table are alone of importance. Top hats do not exist, nor does Guinness's stout. For the "artist," the purveyor of fine feelings, the presbyter of sensibility, the only thing that exists is the effect of the appearance of those things upon his emotions, that is to say upon his nerves; for he will not allow his rationality to have any part in the business. The senses are a kind of reason, said St. Thomas Aquinas, meaning that they lead us to reality. But to the modern artist the senses do not lead outwards to a real universe and a real God, but inwards to a more and more evanescent personality and eventually to its real vanishing point.

On the other hand, while the artists are proclaiming the visibility of "art" more and more loudly, the tendency among industrialists is to make its invisibility more and more imperative and necessary. You could not help having the expression of human sensibility in the work of pre-industrial stone carvers and every other sort of workman; but there was no talk about it and no need of any. There is nothing else but the expression of human sensibility in the works of these modern "artists"; and there is every need to make the most of it. But there can be no legitimate expression of human sensibility in the products of industrialism, therefore it is necessary that all imitations of it shall be carefully excluded. Machine printing must be invisible—in the sense that no "artistic business" must be allowed to obtrude itself between author and reader. Architecture must be invisible in the sense that it must no longer be possible to say of a building: some architect hath done this. And architectrual sculpture must be invisible—in the sense that no "plastic" business must obtrude itself between the idea to be conveyed and its reception by the spectator; for there can no longer be any architectural sculpture whose business is purely ornamental, any more than there can be typographical enrichment in books. Ornamental enrichment cannot be produced by machines.

This tendency to reasonable plainness in industrial products is obviously all to the good; but we may deplore the division of the human race which has made it necessary. On the one hand are the "artists" whose work is nothing but a kind of psychological exhibitionism, on the other are the "workmen" whose work is nothing but the produce of a human ant-heap.

CHAPTER VII

The Beautiful and the Ugly

THE beautiful thing is that which being seen pleases (*Id quod visum placet*).* This is an obvious fact. It is neither a definition of beauty nor of beautifulness, it is simply a statement of fact. And of course the ugly is that which being seen, if it can be seen, displeases. This is a fact also. The only difficulty is with regard to the meaning attached to the words "seen" and "pleases." Let us take it that the word "seen" means "sensed," i.e. obtained, got hold of, acquired through the senses. Man being a sort of "gaze hound" naturally talks in terms of the visual faculty although his other senses, especially that of hearing, are also contributory to his knowledge. But, obviously, other things besides objects of eyesight are objects of beauty; so the word "seen" means also heard, touched, tasted, and smelt. Sight and hearing, not being sources of localised pleasure (a pleasant sight or sound does not make you say your eye or your ear feels nice—whereas smooth skin feels nice to the finger, good apples taste nice in the mouth, and a sweet smell is nice in the nose), are called the disinterested senses and the idea of beauty is more closely associated with sight and hearing than with the other senses because the pleasure obtained from good sights or good sounds is not associated in our memories with the well-being of the organs involved. But all pleasure is pleasure

* St. Thomas Aq., *Summa Theologica*, Part I, Q. 5 and 4.

of the mind. To feel well is to think so. Feeling well is as much a state of mind as feeling happy.

But when we say the beautiful thing is that which being seen pleases we must remember that it is the *thing* which is seen. It is remarkably easy to look at a thing and not see it. Confronted by the painted portrait of a friend most people hardly, that is to say only with great difficulty, see the painting itself. They only see a reminder of their friend. They judge the thing as a likeness only and not at all as a painting. They are still entitled to say that the portrait pleases them or does not, but in that case they should remember that what they are saying is simply that it is or is not a pleasing portrait and that they have not said whether or no it is a pleasing painting.

"What I ask of a painting," said the French painter, Maurice Denis, "is that it should look like paint." But several centuries of insistence upon verisimilitude as being the highest quality of good painting have obfuscated our minds and filled us with the quite silly notion that everything reminiscent of natural appearance should be a faithful facsimile. We suppose that a portrait of a man of flesh and blood should produce the illusion that that man is standing before us. On the contrary it is better to say that things should look like what they are —that a stone carving should look like stone, a painting like paint, instrumental music like the music of flutes or bassoons or whatever it is, the Tower Bridge like a work of iron engineering and not a medieval castle, and a work of the imagination like a work of the imagination. It may well be that some painters actually set out to produce illusions and to deceive the eye. Let us admit the fact, but let us also admit that there are other and possibly better and more normal kinds of painting. In any case we must be careful to distinguish between the thing seen and the thing of which it reminds us, neither confusing the one with the other nor judging of them as though they were identical.

And when we say the beautiful is that which being seen pleases, let us take it that it is the *mind* which is pleased. In saying this I am not implying a dualism between mind and body. There is, in fact, no pleasure of the body of which we are aware which is not a pleasure of the mind. The most delightful sensation known to man is only called delightful because his mind is delighted —nothing but mind is capable of enjoyment. Though you feel it in your stomach, it is your mind which abhors stomach-ache, and, as far as one can see, a mere dog doesn't *mind* being sick.

But the mind is patient of training. Mortification of the body is primarily mortification of the mind; æsceticism is simply a training of the soul. When vulgar people express themselves as pleased with the things in the shop windows of Oxford Street, the wrong is not in their pleasure but in their vulgarity, that is to say their complete lack of traiing. For an untrained mind is a slipshod mind, a foolish mind, a mind in disorder. Who or what shall order it? And, remembering that the artist is a person who makes things and that he makes things for persons, it is as necessary that the mind of the customer should be trained as it is that the artist's should be. It is no use casting pearls before swine, but the swine should remember that the blame is not all on the thrower.

The whole thing therefore depends on the mind. If all is well with the mind all will be well with the work. No possible standards of beauty and ugliness can be proferred. Beauty is as various as mentality; and ugliness, by which I mean nothing but the privation of beauty, is as various as pain. There is and can be no such thing as pleasure in ugliness. Only let us not identify the beautiful with the prudent. A man may leap gracefully over a precipice. The leap may be beautiful though suicide be imprudent. A man may paint a picture of two lovers united. The picture may be beautiful though its exhibition in public may be imprudent. And, conversely, prudent acts may be conjoined with ugly things. A man may carve a crucifix with fervour and piety and yet make a bad crucifix. For his vulgar untrained mind may have allowed him to suppose that a crucifix is a verisimilitude of an Italian model pretending to be crucified. The crucifix is ugly though his prudence is admirable. And a village maid-servant may, in a perfect spirit of patriotism, deposit her savings of fifteen shillings and ninepence in exchange for a pound's worth of War Loan. Her act is prudent; but usury remains ugly. The beautiful thing is that which being seen pleases. We may leave the matter in those simple terms; we only demand that both artist and customer shall train their minds, that is to say the apparatus by means of which they take pleasure in things.

CHAPTER VIII

Art and Holiness

HOLINESS is moral integrity. But it is more than that, or rather it is more than those words mean in twentieth-century speech, though not more than they mean in strict scholastic use. Holiness is moral integrity become an art, a thing admirable in itself, a thing made. Holiness like art is more than prudence, it is prudence become an end instead of remaining simply a means. Such is the holiness of the saints and there is always a certain gaiety about it, the gaiety of men set free. Utilitarianism is burdensome. To do things always *in that order*, in order that something else should follow, never to do things because they are in themselves worth doing, that is the bore, the burden of mere prudence; that is the burden, the bore of mere piety.

The decay of religion in modern Europe and America is due, more than to anything else, to the decay of holiness. This decay was, under the circumstances of the commercial rule inaugurated in the sixteenth century, of course inevitable. Henceforth the word lost its meaning. It ceased to mean hale and hearty. The holy man was no longer thought of as the whole man. Holiness came to be a partiality, an excess, an overgrowth. It even came to be a cutting off, an æsceticism in the narrow and negative sense of a voluntary privation of sensual enjoyment—to enjoy came to be the reverse of

125

to be holy.* And the holy man was no longer the man fulfilled, the man really enjoying himself, the whole man seeing things whole. He became simply the negative man, the man who did not marry, the man who did not drink beer or wine, the man from whose vocabulary the "best words" were expunged. I say this development was inevitable. Commercial rule is of its nature a rule under which all things are seen as means and none as ends. All things are merchandise and honesty is simply the best policy, the most effectual graft—the British Empire was built on it.

". . . British goods can still be sold the world over for they have the reputation of bearing, and they do in fact bear, hall marks of fine quality and sound workmanship; behind them, too, lies our national reputation for strict business integrity. But if they are to penetrate to the quarters of the globe, it will not be without a clear recognition of the immensely important part played by the financial machine. Here the banks are prepared to

* It is curious to note that while the discoveries of scientists and psychologists are making it clear that our old distinctions between spirit and matter are practically useless, the moralists still go on telling us not to give way to "our lower nature." But appreciation of the lower is a mark of the higher. No other animals enjoy sensuality as human beings do, nor do they reflect upon it; and it is clear that the higher, that is to say the more morally developed and intellectually sensitive races and individuals enjoy and reflect upon sensuality more than do lower races or individuals. "The senses are a kind of reason," and the appreciation of the sensual is the mark of human rationality and not of animal instinct. But we are now organising human labour so that the work of the ordinary industrial workman is becoming more and more purely material and insensitive and that of the independent workman, the "artist," more and more purely spiritual. The psychologist discovers that the distinction between matter and spirit is difficult to discover. The industrialist arranges things so that it is difficult for the labourer to be anything but a materialist (hence Marxian Communism) and difficult for the "artist" to be anything but a dealer in immaterial psychologisms.

co-operate with all the services at their command . . . under the banker's hands lie all the controls . . ." So runs the leaflet on the *Financial Machinery of Exports and Imports*, published by the Westminster Bank and "Never in the whole course of our rough island story," proclaims the British Institute of Industrial Art, in one of its first leaflets, "has it been more necessary than it is now to swell the volume of foreign trade. To this end the collaboration of artists with manufacturers is essential in order that the selling quality of British goods may be enhanced" (or words to that effect). Honesty must be supplemented by art, the sales cannot otherwise be maintained.

But holiness is of its nature disinterested and it is here that the bridge, the common ground between art and religion is to be seen. Art in its first simple meaning is simply skill; but among men it is the skill of men; among men it is skill in making; it is skill in making things. Man has never been, "rough island story" or otherwise, merely the labourer beloved as an employee ("one loves one's men") by men of commerce. He has always been the artist, the person who, having freewill (at least in his imagination—I leave the proof to the philosophers) and therefore the power of choice, has not been content with things as being merely serviceable but has always desired to make things representative of his freedom. I am free, child of God, heir also. This walking-stick, this building, this poem shall also be free, "on its own" and no mere chattel. This was the attitude of mind, towards himself and towards his work, which prevailed everywhere at all times, as much before Christianity as afterwards. What, we may claim, Christianity did

was to make the thing explicit—"not to destroy but to
fulfil." We groaned under "the law"; it was an unnatural state, a state contrary to man's nature. "Now
we are free. . . ." And what we claim commercialism
has done is, precisely, to re-establish "the law." It has
reaffirmed the servility both of men and things. It has
thrown men back under the yoke of the mean; the
technical has overwhelmed the poetic. Not to make but
to do is the lot of man under the reign of money-men.

The disinterestedness of the artist, the maker, the
responsible workman is the thing which makes him
friend and brother to the saint, the holy man. The saint
is the disinterested man; the artist is the disinterested
workman. Their disinterestedness is their common
ground. "Art and religion," we say, and we yoke the
two words as though they might not naurally be found
together. In fact they cannot be separated. Religion,
the word, shorn of all its sectarian associations, means
simply the experience of God. Man, the artist, is man
experiencing himself as God, collaborating with God in
creating, his imagination formative of things and not
formed by them. You cannot separate art and religion.
The religious man is simply man, the artist is simply
religious man turned workman.

But religion under commercial rule having become an
affair of sects and secret societies, now only means the
tenets of this or that sect. Religious art, therefore, now
means nothing more than things made in accordance with
the requirements of this or that recognised religious
organisation. But this is all wrong. Religious art does
not mean the art of depicting the gods or the saints; nor
does it mean the art of decorating churches. Such things

are to-day generally not religious at all. They are to-day generally the produce of commercial enterprise, factory products, the produce of men who are not men, having become mere "hands," men who do not experience themselves as gods, whose freewill is denied and whose works, being without faith are as dead as faith is dead without works. Religion and Industrialism are incompatible. Religious art cannot be produced in factories.

Religion is the experience of God. Religious art is the work of men experiencing themselves as God—"I have said ye are gods." Holiness is the fruit of religion. The holy man sees himself whole, and gaiety is the mark of holiness. Holiness and therefore gaiety are the marks of religious art. "Be you also holy"—that is the whole law and the prophets.

The reader must now sort out for himself the difference between the gay and the frivolous, between solemnity and gloom, between asceticism and despair. There is a sort of grim gaiety very noticeable even among those most heroic and stern men, the Jesuit priests who were martyred by the American Indians in the seventeenth century. There is a lightness and gaiety in the self-immolation of St. Rose of Lima. It is notorious that the Blessed Thomas More laughed on the scaffold. There is a sort of bright-eyed shiningness about the solemn chant of the Mass which is commonly absent in the music of musical comedies. There is more sprightliness in the paintings of Cimabue than in all the boudoir art of Park Lane and Pompeii. There is a sort of dancing spirit in Sir Christopher Wren which is quite absent in the architects of the Gothic Revival though they proposed to revive the gayest of all styles of building and he to

E

revive the most pompous. There is more gaiety in candle-light than in all the lights of Piccadilly. There is more gloom and despair in a commercial Father Christmas than in all the verses of the *Dies Irae*.

It is impossible to put the thing too strongly or strongly enough. What is the mark which distinguishes the good from the bad, in works as in men? Holiness is the only word for it.

I say simply that holiness is the name for that quality in things by which we judge them good. Its full meaning escapes definition in words. It is a spiritual thing; it must be apprehended by the spirit. And I am not speaking of holiness as a moral quality. Holiness is not a moral quality at all. It is above and beyond prudence. It is loveliness itself. It is the loveliness of the spirit.

The Author and Publishers wish to acknowledge their indebtedness to the Editors of the *New English Weekly* and *Blackfriars* for permission to reprint these Essays which first appeared in their Journals—that by Rayner Heppenstall on Anonymity as being an admirable reinforcement of the author's argument and that by G. M. Turnell on the School of Baudelaire as being a good example of the specialised study referred to in the text.

APPENDIX I

The Question of Anonymity

HALF-WAY up that breathless, rather absurd tower of Strasbourg Cathedral may be seen the vandal name of Goethe, who came there in the prosecution of certain lecheries, but nowhere can his name be found who designed this mad, embarrassed structure nor his indeed who devised, to his misery and unacknowledgeable renown, its fantastical clock. We have Goethe's name, which is irrelevant, and we have countless other names, which are not even interesting. But we do not know the architects of our great cathedrals. Medieval painting, music, poetry, also are anonymous. A few names that we have, unearthed here and there by scholars, are commonly problematical, and certainly we know more names of minor officials than of major poets. Only with the onset of Renascence No. 1 do we meet the Artist, and Chaucer is our first Poet writ large, one who had no small amount of self-consciousness too in the face of posterity. In the Middle Ages proper, artist was simple artisan. That he served capital Art with passion, with high and difficult technique, with stern patience—this we cannot doubt. But he had no spurring from Glory nor even, it seems, great guerdon.

Meditating on such things to-day, we grow sentimental. We are puzzled also. That a man should make a cathedral and not put his name on the time-list—what heartbreak devotion. That men should acclaim some swaggering bombard-baron and not fête their artists—how barbarous. Yet surely this, and not our modern condition in which even I may sign a short essay, is the normal. A high art, considerable by any standards, goes back with the Sumerians as far, to our certain knowledge, as 3500 B.C. Yet there are no names of artists until the Glory that was Greece becomes uncomfortable. Exquisite work was done by Egyptian artists in tombs where even the contemporary eye was not expected. And the major art of India is anonymous, even in modern times. The ages in which artists have claimed public recognition, much less pronounced for immortality, cover an almost insignificant piece of time. Only in the modern world is it Personality that counts, in Art as in Business. Only for a little while have we demanded the love-letters of our artists and been unable to like or dislike a poem until we know who has written it.

If we ponder this we ask questions which lay bare the very nervequick of art. Not of æsthetics, but of art functions, the definition of cultures. We do not ask What is Art? as who cries *O Altitudo* or as Sean O'Casey's man bibulously questioning What is the stars?—what IS the stars? But we demand what it may be in the structure and quality of a society, a culture, which determines that sublime art shall be produced in complete obscurity or that passionate art shall be produced with decent reticence or that interesting art shall be produced with much gesticulation—for this ratio of attributes seems justified. And a tentative answer will inevitably be in terms of function. We shall surmise that an anonymous art is somehow intrinsic to the basic needs of a society, that an art whose authors are named with honour may be a wholly valid art and yet is external to the deepest social movements, and that a highly self-conscious art is a functionless art, the produce of men who, as artists, are set apart from society.

Surely enough until Athens first cast up great names art in the Ancient World was an integral service of religion. So it was also in the close-built socio-religious structure of Medieval Europe. And so it is in modern India. To the Hindu, art is one means of peeling away *Maya*, the Appearance, and of fixing in durant symbol some facet of immanent godhead, the Reality. The artist is a craftsman attached to the temples. Art is hereditary, a caste function, and works by traditional canon.

But we do not solve our problem by saying that in all times, except a few intruded centuries of self-consciousness, art has been the servant of religion, and that anonymous art is essentially religious art. For what do the terms mean? Surely Blake's art is essentially religious. So indeed is that of Lawrence. And these are far from anonymity. Hieratic is probably a fitter term than Religious for the great ages of unsigned art. It is not true that Sumerian or Medieval or Hindu art is more wholly the expression of a religious conception than that of Lawrence or Blake or indeed that of any artist intense enough to build up his own life within a religious conception. The difference is that Babylonia, like the Church of the Middle Ages, like the Hindus, had a religious conception equated to the social conception. Society moved within the religious framework, which was a binding ethic, both an index and a sanction for all activity. There was no separation of religion from philosophy and science, of art from politics and entertainment, no division of Truth into many notional categories. There was one ideological framework for all processes of living. And art was ritual. Art is perhaps always that, but here it was rital for a truly welded and whole society, the heraldry of a fully integrated public mode of belief and behaviour. This is the very definition of a culture, and within such a culture tradition defines itself. But to-day tradition is a subject for metaphysical discussion, and our culture—if we may still claim to have or to BE one—is more closely defined by dress fashions than by art.

In our time, Art is the *Reductio ad Absurdum* of Itself. Less epigrammatically, contemporary works of art and the relations between art and society are such as to render untenable any hypothesis singly proposed for the nature and function of art. Even the non-committal Marxian view would need to be thoroughly overhauled and redialecticised before application. In other circumstances, art may well be a reflection of ruling-class ideology, but the position of the Superstructure becomes rather precarious when there is no body of people sufficiently large, homogeneous and cleanly stratified to be described as a class at all, and when those groups which are least equivocally said to rule have no ideology intensive enough to need reflection in art. It is not that society has entirely ceased to be interested in art, but simply that cultural feeling tends to base itself rather on the sentiments of the stock exchange and to find adequate ritual expression in the kaleidoscopic pageantry of dress fashions, or, to the extent that artistic activity has a cultural rôle at all, in certain mushroom art-forms explicitly recognised as pure diversion, so that art proper has no internal function but becomes a branch of the tourist industry.

Among artists, and to some degree among cultivated people generally, as we may learn by reading *Scrutiny*, there is a feeling that such a state of affairs is unsatisfactory. And yet, logical conclusion as this state is of the whole process of personalisation, very few people, artists in particular, would whole-heartedly seek outlet by a return to cultural anonymity. They would feel such return to be a complete negation of Art—as indeed it is, for Art with the capital means that near traditional hinterland only, becoming steadily more barren as it approaches the present seaboard.

Putting aside, however, the fact that so many artists to-day are more concerned to BE Poet or Painter than to create works of art, the immediate question for serious people would normally be whether anonymous art is likely to be intrinsically superior to signed art. But that is an impossible question. There are no standards for comparing the Opus 111 with a Sumerian statue, and in any case Beethoven represents merely a phase in the process of transition from Ur to Mr. Shaw. The question may be proposed more broadly. Will anonymous art tend to define a culture more generally pleasing to persons of æsthetic interests? And there it is possible to submit an affirmative. Anonymous art is necessarily art subdued to a central non-æsthetic purpose, a social or socio-religious conception, and however much we, trained to think of art in terms of personality, to define art, at least implicitly, as self-expression, and to rate æsthetic values as somehow above social values—however much we may resent the thought of any such subordination of art to a non-æsthetic purpose, we must realise, though it may be contemptuously labelled hieratic rather than religious and political perhaps rather than hieratic, that this centripetal force makes bad art impossible. Bad art is always to be defined as completely secular art and as such would be ruled inevitably out of a centralised cultural programme. True, this natively artistic argument for anonymity is purely a negative one. But it is cogent, for the evil symptoms to-day are not in the lack of good art but in excess of the bad. And it is doubtful if any positive argument could be advanced for signed art, except by those whose definition of art would be, in moments of complete and lucid honesty, the Activities of an Artist.

Unfortunately, in the absence of any compelling central conception, it is possible only to register sympathy with the Idea of anonymity and go on signing. Those who would play a cultural rôle in their age must give their talents to the true cultural industries—dance music, the cinema, dress designing, advertising, and the daily press—while They who cleave to that stale wench Art posture before the curtain and roar out their *Vesti la giubba* in ever more tremulous tenor voices.

RAYNER HEPPENSTALL

APPENDIX II

*The School of Baudelaire**

IT would hardly be possible to over-estimate the significance for the modern world of the supposed antithesis between Idea and Reality. It leads necessarily to the conclusion that we can have no conceptual knowledge of the real and that therefore personal experience is the sole reality. This theory probably did more than anything else to undermine medieval unity and to divide culture into an immense number of tiny independent cells.

The influence of subjective philosophy on poetry is important, for the poetry of a period is usually determined by prevailing conceptions of reality. Consider the position of the medieval poet as compared with that of the modern. The medieval poet belonged to a society united by a common faith. The materials of his art were the things he had in common with his fellow-men—the Faith, and the outer world as given in sense-experience. The importance of the outer world must be emphasized. No one denies that the invisible world played a large part in medieval art, but the basis was the visible world. The poet proceeded from nature to the supernatural. The data of his experience were furnished by the visible concrete world. The modern poet, on the contrary, is an inhabitant of a world where there are no common intellectual principles, no common spiritual background and—perhaps the most important of all—no great measure of agreement about the nature of the external world. The poet is left to interpret everything for himself.

* Extracts from an essay in *Blackfriars*, January, 1934, by permission of the author.

The outcome has been the shifting of the poet's vision from the outer world to "the world within." Man has become the centre of the universe, and modern art has for the most part been concerned not with what is *seen* but with what is *felt*. Instead of investigating the world in which he is placed —*la sainte réalité*, as Claudel has magnificently called it— and seeking to penetrate to that deeper reality which is revealed to the artist's intuition, the modern poet is only concerned with the emotions that this world rouses in him. (This is the only intelligible meaning of "self-expression" in art.) Instead of a common, we get a purely personal vision. In such a world it is naturally difficult to control or test the artist's experience, to decide whether one interpretation of the universe is truer or more valuable than another.

The modern poet then is faced with the problem of finding a new common basis of experience. In general poets have chosen one of two alternatives. They have either abandoned the attempt altogether, or they have sought the new common basis in man himself. Thus we get on the one hand the poetry of escape, on the other a new realism—a compromise between romanticism and naturalism.

Escape was the "solution" of the romantics. They turned away from the visible world and constructed a dream-world, or "returned to nature." This fictitious world possessed the unity which was sadly lacking in the actual world. It had another advantage too. The Romantic Movement was contemporary to the rise of Industrialism. Now one of the most perplexing and difficult problems for the modern poet has been the rapid transformation of nature through the growth of the great manufacturing centres. The dream-world of the romantics provided something stable and unchanging in the midst of change. The inevitable result of such an outlook is that the poet gets completely out of touch with the living world. He is deprived of the normative influence of society and he comes finally to express only those feelings that make him different from other men. His work is therefore nothing but a record of abnormal states of mind which must remain incomprehensible to the world at large.

*   *   *

The new modes of feeling, the fresh outlook, that Baudelaire and his disciples introduced into poetry are first apparent in their choice of subject. They write of things which cannot possibly be reconciled with conventional romantic theories of the "beautiful" and the "poetic." In poems like *Une Charogone* and *Vénus Anadyomène* we meet almost for the first time that delight in the ugly which is so much a part of modern poetry—as though poets were bent on showing that they could make poetry out of things hitherto regarded as in themselves unpoetic. Their work marks a definite change in European sensibility, and we can apply to them words used by T. S. Eliot to describe the English Metaphysical Poets, "They possessed a mechanism of sensibility which could devour any kind of experience." They are interested in things like decaying corpses, epileptics in cheap lodging-houses, drunkenness and all the squalid horror of city-life. Baudelaire specialises in prostitution, and Rimbaud has been called—not altogether unjustly—the poet of the latrines. It is not simply that romantic subjects go by the board; they deliberately ridicule all the things which had previously been admired, and that is the secret of their "wit" which has occupied living critics a good deal.

*   *   *

The modern poet's attitude to his environment is of peculiar interest. The traditional distinction between subject and object is no longer so clear-cut as of old. The external world is no longer distinct from the men who move in it, it has become merged in their experiences. The more we read their work the more apparent it becomes that their primary interest was neither in the real world nor in the world of appearances, but in the happenings in their own minds. Baudelaire, for instance, seldom brings his mind to bear *directly* on a concrete object. He is concerned with it in relation to himself, with its impact on his own sensibility instead of its place in a general scheme. He sees things not as they are, but in terms of his reactions to them. It is not easy to describe the process which is different from the romantic poet's projection of his own feelings into nature. But in reading Baudelaire one has the impression that the poet is deliberately and consciously distorting what he has seen (often to the point of caricature) in order to intensify, in an altogether extraordinary degree, the emotion associated with the actual scene, or with the materials out of which it was constructed. In many cases the result is an emotional reaction out of all proportion to the original stimulus, which is apparently what the poet aims at. We certainly see this process at work in Baudelaire's description of the dead beggar:

> Les jambes en l'air, comme une femme lubrique,
>   Brûlante et suant les poisons,
> Ouvrait d'une façon nonchalante et cynique
>   Son ventre plein d'exhalaisions.

Or in this description of a Paris dawn:

> Une mer de broillards baignait les édifices
> Et les agonisants dans le fond des hospices
> Poussaient leur dernier râle en hoquets inégaux.
> Les débauchés rentraient, brisés par leurs travaux.

These are extreme examples chosen to bring out the point. Baudelaire's attitude towards the external world reveals what is perhaps the most striking characteristic of the modern mind—a complete despair of finding any ultimate order or unity in the structure of the universe. For him the chaos is final. The medieval artist loved concrete things, whereas the modern regards them with a mixture of fascination and disgust. He faces the real only because it will procure for him new sensations. It is also a means of self-revelation. *One of Baudelaire's triumphs was that he managed, by establishing new contacts with the outer world, to turn other facets of his own personality to the light.*

This brings us to Baudelaire's other innovation. I have said that his chief interest was in the workings of his own mind. His psychological realism is at once his most significant contribution to poetry and his most effective criticism of the romantic aberration. His experiment of making the outer world a means to an end was brilliantly successful; it enabled him not simply to lay bare fresh ranges of feeling, but to reveal the modern mind to itself in a new way. Instead of seeking a common basis for experience in the world as presented to the senses, he tries by delving into himself to come to fresh common ground within. That is the modern poet's solution of the problem before him. Thus the central point of Baudelaire's work consists in a certain movement of the mind turned in upon itself, and its end would seem to be the discovery of an absolute self that is hidden beneath the different layers of mind.

*   *   *

This turning of the mind inward is also a last attempt made by the artist to discover in himself—in the structure of his own inner consciousness—the unity that he has failed to discern in the world outside him. Unfortunately the inner consciousness is nothing but a meeting-place for the disconnected stream of thoughts and feelings to which the artist's life has been reduced by excessive introspection. It simply mirrors the chaos outside him. Then, almost by accident, the problem solves itself. It is in the common despair brought about by their failure to discover a coherent world-order that the poets are at one. There is no common vision, only a common emotion. *Je finis*, wrote Rimbaud, *par trouver sacré le désordre de mon esprit.* He speaks for them all. One of the criteria proposed by contemporary critics is that poetry should "express the ways of feeling . . . of one fully alive to his own time." In other words, the poet is expected to express a certain *emotional state* which the critic believes to be proper to our time. This means that an outlook, which is due to the changed relation between man and the external world and which is necessarily relative to a given period of history, is erected into an absolute standard.*

* It is interesting to note than an attempt is being made by the most recent movement in English poetry to escape from a position of complete subjectiveness by seeking a common basis in political doctrine. The poets would make of political faith a substitute for the religious faith which formed a common bond in the Middle Ages.

                                                      G. M. TURNELL

Bibliography

Thomas Aquinas   *Summa Theologica*, Part 1.Q.5
Thomas Aquinas   *De Regimine Principum*
John Ruskin   *Unto this Last*
Jacques Maritain   *Art and Scholasticism*
Jacques Maritain   *The Frontiers of Poetry*
Christopher Dawson   *Progress and Religion*
Ananda Coomaraswamy   *Introduction to the Art of Eastern Asia*
Ananda Coomaraswamy   *The Transformation of Nature in Art*
Clive Bell   *Art*
Herbert Read   *Art Now*
Eric Gill   *Art Nonsense*
Eric Gill   *Clothes*
Eric Gill   *Beauty looks after Herself*
MacNair Wilson   *Monarchy and Money Power*
Christopher Hollis   *The Breakdown of Money*
Julien Benda   *The Great Betrayal*
Nicholas Berdyaev   *The End of Our Time*
Prince Kropotkin   *Fields, Factories and Workshops*
W. R. Lethaby   *Medieval Art*
J. & R. Hammond   *History of the Agricultural Labourer*
G. G. Coulton   *Art and the Reformation*

Index